AF580161

root

i want to

and

we GOT GAME!

NUL 732Y

root
Conway Lloyd Morgan
aveditionrockets

'The cause follows the effect, or the reason for the journey is a consequence of the journey' (Jorge Luis Borges, Coleridge's Flower)
The central idea for the Rockets series was to explore the work of individual design groups in new ways. Not just through a showcase, interesting as that is to the design community, nor via the formal monograph, useful as that may be to the design historian. Rather I felt the books should represent some interaction between an author/editor and the designers concerned. A discourse, not a commentary, a joint development of ideas and concepts against a background of completed work that crossed traditional boundaries. One in which the author's text would not attempt to describe the work case by case – as if the values of visible work would not appear until touched by words – but would instead provide a parallel context, in this case through coincident texts.
The idea for this approach comes from my friend Jean Nouvel, who used a fictive text – which he wrote himself – to preface a description of his INIST building. But if the inspiration came from Jean, the execution – with all its attendant faults – is entirely my own.
Conway Lloyd Morgan
Series editor

Wilma had always worried about the bomb. Sorry, the Bomb. Not just Their Bomb, of course, but Our Bomb as well.

'What'll happen if they drop the bomb now?' she'd ask Norm as they drove ten blocks down in the pick-up to buy the day's goods in the market. 'Listen,' Norm would say, 'if they hit the centre of the city, out here at the diner we have a full load of food, we just head up away from the city, go into the hills: we'll be all right.' Norm doubted that the Soviet High Command had targeted his small city among many others, but, what the hell, he loved his wife: make her happy, let it go. Somewhere at the back of his mind he remembered the civil defense lessons: perhaps even the hills wouldn't be safe from, what was it, radiation, but still, what the hell, she was silly to worry. 'That's what he'd say on the good days: when he was moody he'd just mutter 'they are going to start the war while we are at the market, are they,' and hunch down over the wheel again. What could they do about it, after all. 'When the bomb that drops on you, gets your friends and neighbours too, they'll be no one around left to grieve, so we'll all go together when we go...' He hadn't liked the song that had come in with a batch of records for the juke-box and had in fact removed it deliberately, but the refrain and words still ran in his head. Norm drove the pick-up loaded with bags of onions and potatoes, cases of relish and cans of Coke resolutely back to the diner: bomb or no bomb, they had a business to run. Besides, it was Thursday, and the spacemen would be coming in: Wilma liked worrying them about the Bomb.

He called them the spacemen because, years before, they'd picked up the signals from Sputnik on their ham radio, been one of the first in the States to do so, long before the professional guys worked out that Sputnik was deliberately using a ham radio frequency. Al and George announced the fact in the diner that evening, brought in a tape recording: that was a Thursday, so they came back every Thursday. Ham radio they might call it, but their set-up was, Norm thought, pretty professional. Al had been a signalman with the Marines in Korea, and George had worked as a radio artificer on a carrier in the Navy during his service. Often they'd talk about the foreign signals they picked up and the guys in Australia and other out of state places (Al had once said their ham friend in Australia was 'pretty out of state,' and Wilma had laughed at that.) But they really loved the space race, and had followed the Mercury, Gemini and Apollo missions with passion: if there was a space broadcast going out on a Thursday, they'd insist Norm put it on the television in the bar, even if the Diamondbacks were playing that evening. Despite this, for he loved his baseball, Norm had got kind of interested himself, and he had surely felt for those guys in Apollo Thirteen: funny they hadn't skipped the number, like they did in the floor numbers of some of the San Francisco hotels, Norm thought. Al had said that was because the astronauts weren't superstitious, goddamit, they were professionals, heroes even: George, on the other hand, had told him all the pilots he'd ever met, even the carrier pilots, were all daft about superstitions: some would even refuse to fly without a lucky mascot like a rabbit's foot or a medallion they had.

And Wilma would talk to them about the Bomb: 'were They going to put the Bomb in space?' she'd ask, and 'how far can Their big rockets get now? They're better than ours, aren't they?' And George and Al would josh her about it. 'Wilma,' they'd say 'we've volunteered you for the Moon settlement program, you'll be safe there.' Funnily enough, Wilma wasn't frightened of space: she'd kinda known the Apollo Thirteen guys would get back OK, but, still, she worried about the Bomb.

But that Thursday something changed. The Ruskies had done it again. They'd put up another satellite, but not just a bunch of radios and cameras and stuff. This one people could live in. A space station, the papers had said, a true satellite, like the moon. Norm was waiting to hear what the spacemen said about it, and called a greeting to them as they came in. 'Hi, Norm,' they both replied, going to their usual booth. 'Hey, Wilma,' George had said when she came over for their order, 'guess what?' 'About what,' she asked 'you guys not taking the Blue Plate this evening?' 'No,' said George, 'about the Soviets' satellite.' Wilma looked worried. 'Yea,' said Al, 'it's called Soyuz.' 'Soyuz,' said Wilma cautiously. 'It means "unity" in Russian. Did you know that?' George explained.

Wilma came back to the bar and turned to Norm. 'It's called Soyuz,' she said, as if Norm hadn't heard 'and that means unity.' She paused. 'That's a good sign isn't it? So I guess that means everything is all right now.' And that's why Wilma stopped worrying about the Bomb.

vega4

now you ignore me
i'm here by myself
i just wanna be happy
i'm drifting away, violently

Lyrics from 'Drifting away violently' from the album Satellites by Vega4.

PED
XING

love it was an after thought
in the world outside
but i'll find it when i fly

Lyrics from 'Love Breaks Down' from the album Satellites by Vega4.

WARNING: OTHER STANDS MAY CAUSE DROWSINESS

DO NOT EXCEED RECOMMENDED DOSAGE

DO NOT USE AFTER 05 SEPTEMBER 2000

IF SYMPTOMS PERSIST CONSULT A DOCTOR

STORE IN A COOL DRY PLACE

The Specialists

The Specialists®

The Specialists
PC Titles
The Specialists
he Specialists
onsole Titles
The Specialists

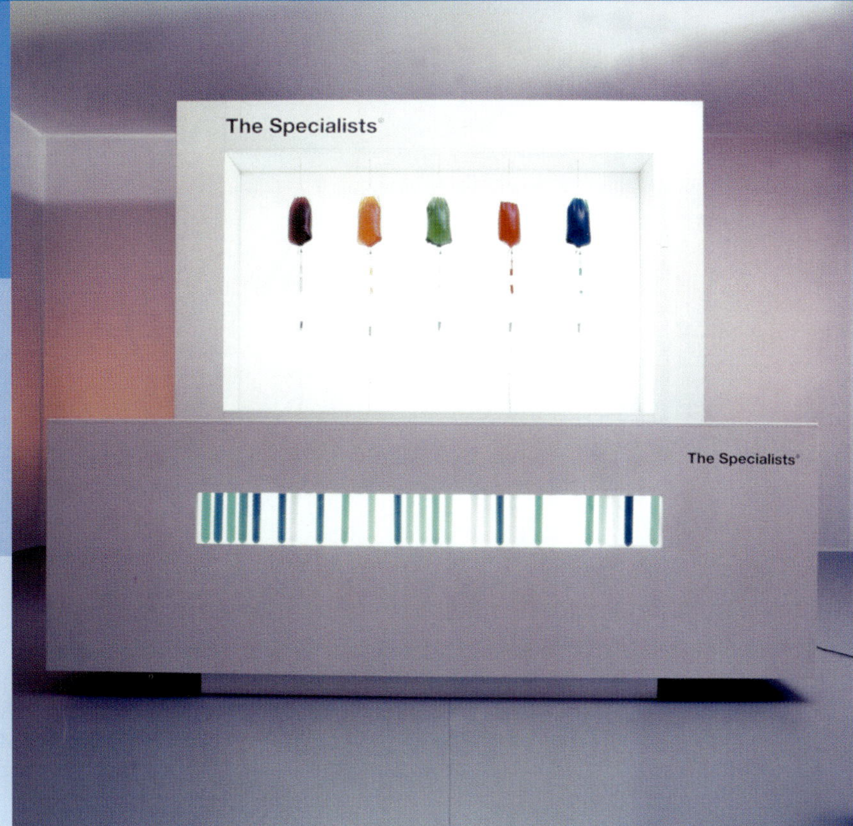
The Specialists
The Specialists

The Specialists

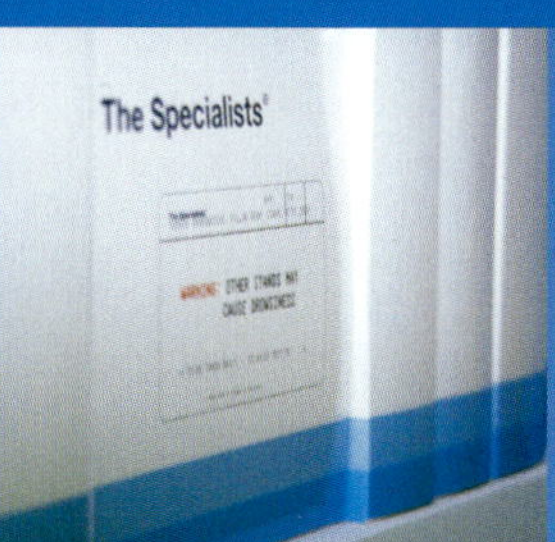
The Specialists

DO NOT EXCEED THE RECOMMENDED DOSAGE
The Specialists
MAY CAUSE UNWANTED SIDE EFFECTS
IF SYMPTOMS PERSIST

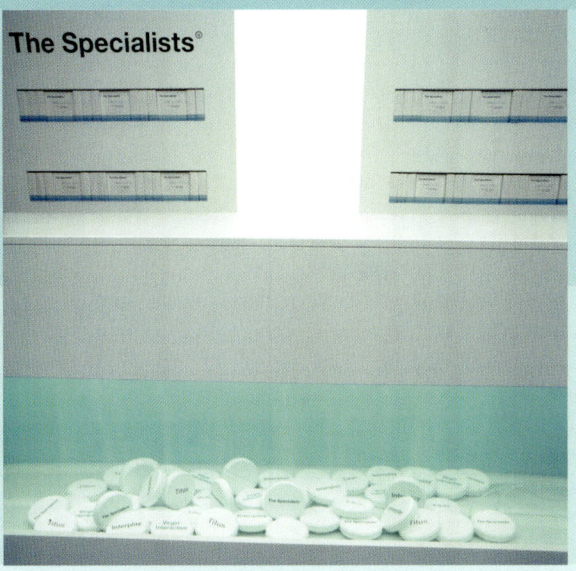
The Specialists®

The Specialis
Product Room
Toilets

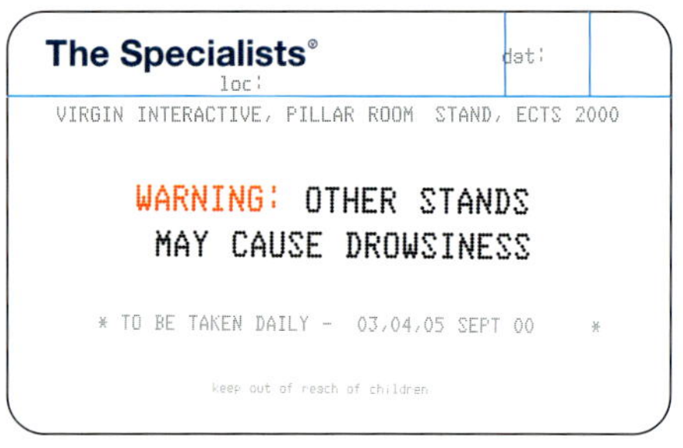

Visit **The Specialists**®

03/04/05 September - Virgin Interactive, Titus, Interplay. Pillar Room. ECTS 2000. **Appointment Only**

We were sitting in the jazz club in the basement that Tuesday, as we did most Tuesdays, listening to Bernd paying homage to be-bop and Ellen singing her own so crafted and so crafty songs. And we were arguing about live jazz. Something that we all supported, of course, live jazz, or we'd hardly be there. But the argument was whether we should, could, ought or ought not to listen to recorded jazz, and especially to recorded contemporary jazz which used electronic effects. We'd been arguing about this about once a month since Clint Eastwood released his film Bird, on Charlie Parker, so I guess Bernd playing be-bop was bound to bring it up again. Of course, as we'd been having the argument for ages, some of the arguments were getting a bit esoteric, even among jazz fans. Petra had developed a complex and wholly existential position on this, based on the unheard music of Billy Bowden. She argued that because Billy Bowden had played, and only played live, live jazz was the only way. But she used Sartre's existentialism for this, not Heidegger's, and was not to be countered by the argument that since no-one alive had ever heard Bowden play, perhaps he had in fact never played live, or even played at all. (My alternative version was that he had played, but only in a studio for some now unknown recording company or system whose output had been either ruthlessly suppressed by white supremacists from Chicago or lost in the San Francisco earthquake.) Not that he was a myth, of course, that would be too simple, and no solution either, since in Sartre's view only the single etre's existence was provable, and then only subjectively, but from that proof the existence, real and mythical at once, of every or, for that matter, any etre could be ineluctably deduced. So Bowden existed as much as I did, or as little. And so live jazz it had to be.

Paul once tried bringing in Godel at this point to see if number theory might elucidate this philosophical impasse. The idea of provable and unprovable statements within a non-linguistic matrix had probably never much influenced Blue Note's policy on re-issues, and it certainly made no impression on Charles – for whom anyway Occam was simply a failed precursor of Gillette. Charles was a computer whiz kid who built multi-media programs for websites and virtual presentations, and for him pre-digital was pre-historic. But he was willing to write what he called a reversibility program, to de-evolutionise music. Suppose, he said, you establish a line that went Marsalis – Coltrane – Getz – Parker – King Oliver – Jellyroll Morton. Turn the order round, analyse the content. Strip out what each had added to their predecessor, and what you were left with was what Bowden would have played. It was that simple, or would have been if we could have ever agreed on a line-up. What about Bix? Why leave out Armstrong? How to fit Bessie Smith in? We were all specialists, and so all knew best. Every time we discussed it Bernd would send over a message to ask us to quiet down so the rest of the audience could hear the music.

And so the undefensible but mildly entertaining arguments went around, all grounded in our enjoyment of live music and our inexplicable certainty that recorded jazz, in particular, lost something in the process. Until Victor came over to the table, as we were having a drink with Bernd and Ellen after the last set. Victor spoke about six languages but claimed not to be have been born in the country of any of them. Taking a piece of paper out of his pocket, he tore four small strips off it and rolled them into tiny balls, and carefully placed one under each of four beer mats lying on the table. With a gesture, he invited Ellen to select an order between the mats. She did so. He tapped on the first one and lifted it: no ball of paper. On the second and lifted it: two balls of paper. Replacing the second he tapped it again and lifted it: nothing underneath. Then he tapped the third: three balls of paper under it. And so on until all four balls of paper disappeared. We cheered and laughed, astonished. Charles's mouth hung open in shock, and he asked Victor to do it again, which he did. I realised that I hadn't seen a live conjuring trick since my childhood, and to see one here, in this dusty basement, performed with no props but the beer mats on the table was utterly compelling. We'd all seen magic shows on the television, but for all their professional flourish, they didn't count. Being there, seeing it happen, knowing it might fail, sharing the pleasure of the performer in front of you: being at the show, that was what counted. 'Now you see what I mean about live music,' said Petra.

CAPCOM
QUICKLY RELIEVES DISCOMFORT

The Specialists*
Game: Dino Crisis 2
Developer: Capcom
IF SYMPTOMS PERSIST CONSULT A SPECIALIST
STORE IN A COOL DRY

i can't

i can't

She had always thought of him as the old professor, though now that she thought about it she wasn't sure if he had really been a professor. He was old, yes, and looked somehow scholarly, as well. She lived a few doors away in the village, and would call in sometimes, and take him a cake or a pot of jam if she'd made some, and talk about the local news. He didn't seem to have many friends, and no-one knew much about him. He'd said once that he'd spent his childhood in Germany, but he didn't talk about himself much, though he was always polite, and interested in her gossip and stories.

One day she'd told him that the doctor's son had got a place at art school, and wanted to be a designer. She had the feeling his parents were pleased about this, but would have been more pleased if it had been law or, even better, medicine. But the old professor interrupted her. 'A designer, eh!' he said, 'so he'll be learning to take a line for a walk.' 'Whatever do you mean?' she asked; it seemed such an odd notion. 'Let me tell you a story,' he replied, and this is what he told her.

When he was a child, his mother had been a teacher in a design school in Germany, before the War, in Dessau, at a school called the Bauhaus. It was a very modern school, and very famous, then and since, but he didn't know that till later and what he remembered most about his life as a small boy had been how different it was. His friends at school – and he'd implied he hadn't had many – lived in homes quite different from his and his mother's house. The friends had patterned carpets, and heavy, dark furniture with soft, coloured cushions. There would be interesting things to look at everywhere, things like china figurines or photographs in ornate frames or knickknacks, souvenirs from other cities in Germany or mementoes of visits to Switzerland or even Venice or Paris. Strange things, sometimes, like the flowers and animals made of clear glass with coloured bits that one friend's mother collected, strange but somehow familiar and friendly.

tea's gone cold
out of bed at all

i'm wondering
why?

i can't
i can't

His own house, in comparison, was bare: plain rugs on the floor, wooden furniture, and no decoration. That wasn't the only difference. His friends would sit down quietly to dinner every evening at six with their mothers and fathers and brothers and sisters, each in their own place. One of his friends even seemed to know what he would have for dinner every day: herring on Fridays, calves' liver on Tuesdays and so on. Dinner at his house could happen any time between six o'clock and midnight, and there might be just his mother and him but more likely there'd be a couple of her students or some of the other teachers: six to ten people at the table was common enough. And they would talk and argue and argue and talk: he's still hear them late at night, after he'd been sent off to bed. He didn't understand half their talk though he recognised the passion in their voices. Anything could set it off: the weather, a book or a picture, even the food.

The food, when it came, was never predictable: sometimes just soup and salad, sometimes an omelette, sometimes a chicken – he liked chicken, but between ten people a chicken wasn't a lot. He was often quite hungry, he remembered, and cold in the winters. And sometimes in the winters meals were awful: not the food, the meals. The soup would arrive, and his mother would ladle it out into bowls, hot and steaming, and just as he was about to begin, one of the guests would say 'Look at the curve of that slice of pepper,' or 'See the way the bubbles slide together' and they'd all be off again, talking about shape and contrast, pure colour, and necessary form, and the metaphysics underlying reality. On and on. And the soup would get cold and colder and he would feel hungrier and hungrier, while the ideas flew in flurries across the table, taking no notice of him. She laughed a little at this story about his mother's odd friends, but he went on.

'One of the teachers I liked very much. He was called Paul and once I shown him some drawings I'd done at school. Paul had looked at them, and I'd explained they were of flowers I'd seen out on a walk. "A drawing isn't 'of' something," Paul had said. "It's just taking a line for a walk." And he said that with such passion and so seriously, and it seemed such a strange thing but a true thing, that I've remembered that moment ever since, and that lovely phrase, "taking a line for a walk".' And the old professor fell silent, as if lost in his memories.

She thought about it when she got home, when she realised the professor had never before told her so much about himself. But what an odd story. And what strange people: she'd never heard of the place. And taking a line for a walk: well, she remembered a bit of geometry, and you couldn't do that – a line was always between two points, she was sure of that. Perhaps she should tell the doctor's son about it, though, just in case. But he probably wouldn't be interested.

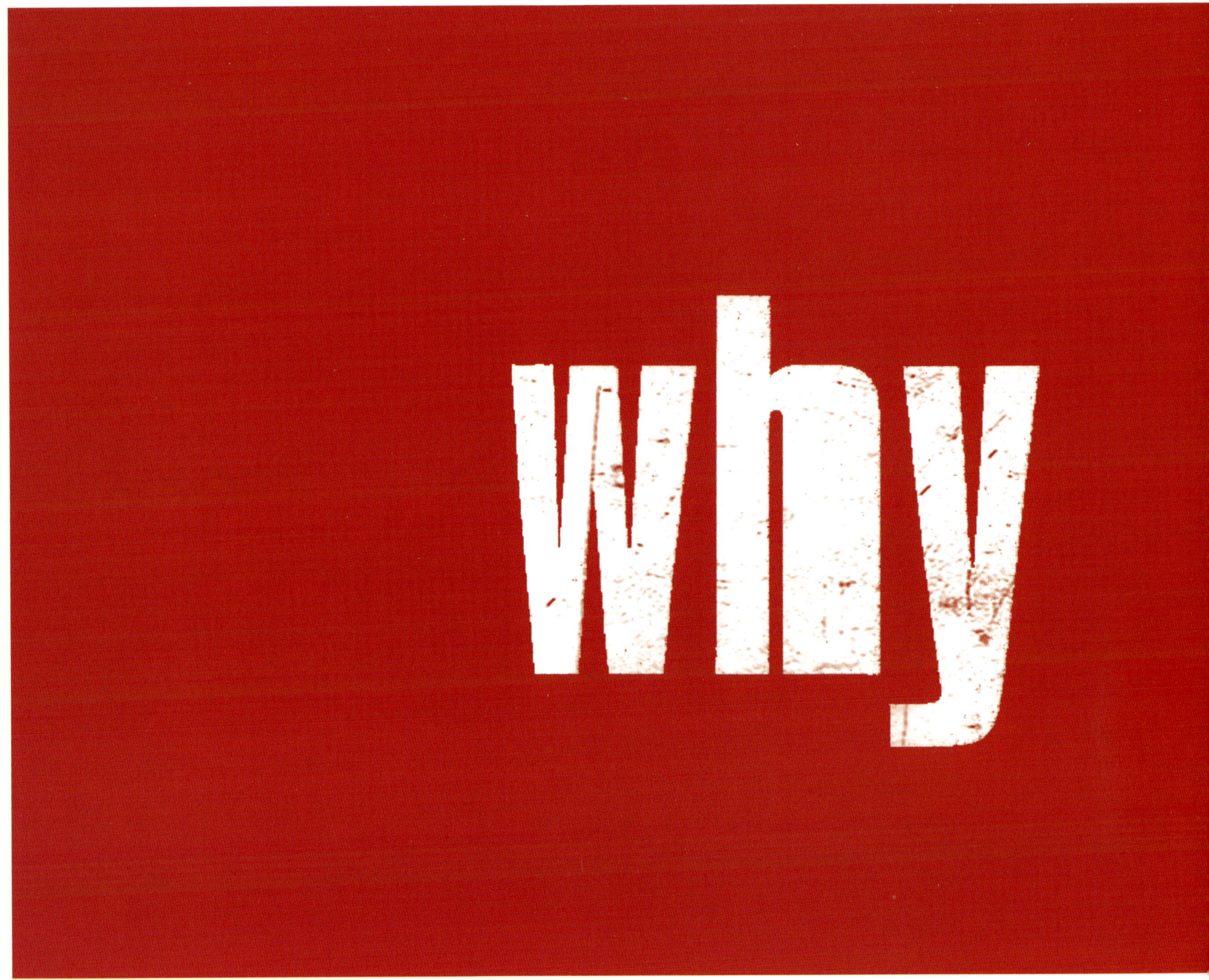
why

here with me
i won't go
go

tea's gone cold

tea's gone cold
until you're resting
out of bed at all

i won't go

i won't go

i can't

i can't

and

here with me

1. Int.
anny's portacabin
ay

anny casually rolls up the money and places it
op pocket just as...

his

Veronique

(eating)

Mmm - un peu sale, mais pas mal. Comment

he does exchange knowing looks. They cast pert little smiles at Raymond.

tu trouves?

and aggravations aired 'never
again'
Hotel Shower............Dawn
'who's idea was this?'

Water thrums against the skin of Raymond's closed eyelids as he sings in the shower - wordless 30's scat. White tiles. Corroded brass fittings. A fresh white towel on the rail. Raymond luxuriates.

Flash cut to:

n his

Veronique

(eating)

Mmm - un peu sale, mais pas mal. Comment

The does exchange knowing looks. They cast pert little smiles at Raymond.

and aggravations aired 'never

'who's idea was this?'

tu trouves?

again'

Who the hell's in charge here...?!

Fais voir. (She peers closer) Non, mais

la, tu as un bout de....Bouge pas.

5. Int. / Women's Car / Day

Water thrums against the skin of Raymond's closed eyelids as he sings in the shower - wordless 30's scat. brass fittings. A fresh white towel on the rail. Raymond luxuriates.

and aggravations aired 'never
again'
'who's idea was this?'
Water thrums against the skin of Raymond's closed eyelids as he sings in the shower - wordless 30's scat. White tiles. Corroded brass fittings. A fresh white towel on the rail. Raymond luxuriates.
Flash cut to:

Steam from the hot soapy water rises.

Skin is becoming wet.
The heat is on.

Dawn

concierge bell for attention...The bel

Water thrums against the skin of Raymond's closed eyelids as he sings in the shower - wordless 30's scat. White tiles. Corroded brass fittings. A fresh white towel on the rail. Raymond luxuriates.

Flash cut to:

stop sulking?

ronique (cont'd)

anny

problem ladies?

first woman

(fact: lots of it ... 20 quid)

Danny (not surprised)

Of course. No problem

eronique

eating)

mm - un peu sale, mais pas mal. Comment

e does exchange knowing looks. They cast polite little smiles at Raymond.

a trouves?

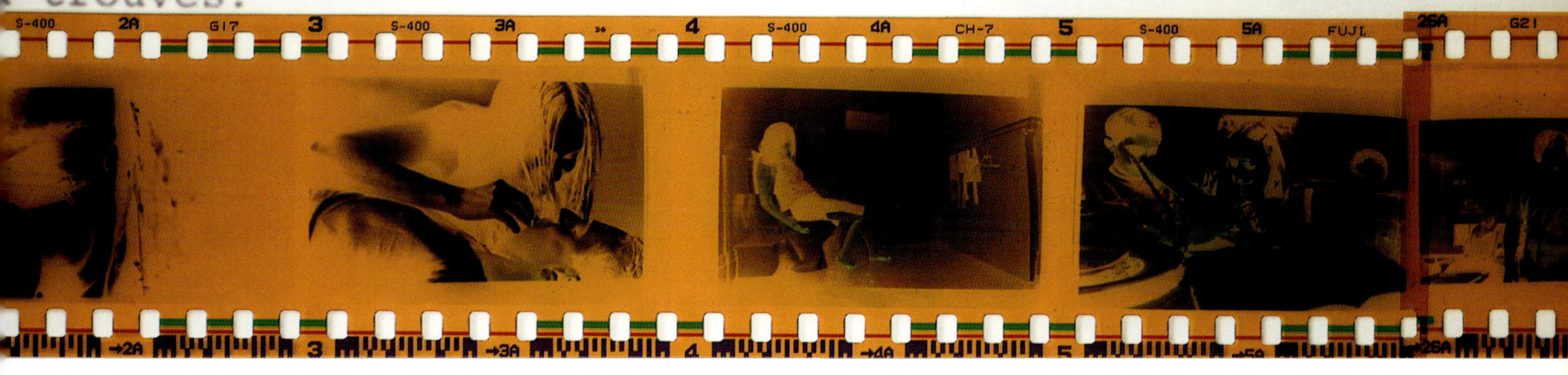

He'd seen it when he was about fifteen late at night on some cable channel, in the middle of some gushy documentary about some actress or other, full of old wrinklies gabbing on about her and Marlon and her and Orson and her and lots of other people who were just as old and wrinkly as they were and he'd never heard of. And then there'd been this shot of the white Cadillac Eldorado Coupe de Ville sliding up to the curb in the middle of a line of black Lincoln Continentals, and her getting out of it, moving like oil on water, and stepping onto the red carpet and turning, her fur coat with the high collar framing her seriously huge hair, and swinging open to show the silver low-cut dress and the barrage of flashguns almost whitening out the whole image. And he'd suddenly thought – that's fame, that is. That's what it's like. And that's what I want.

Funny, he thought, I knew what the car was, exactly: 1965 production model, shown in the Detroit Motorama in 1964, designed by Harley Earl. Who the actress was he'd never known, never bothered to find out. He'd told his art master at school about it, the next day, about how the flash bulbs turned the colour image for moment into something all white but still, sort of, visible. So Mr Joddard the art master had made them play with and paint afterimages for the next lesson: he was OK, the art master, and the afterimages were kind of cool, but he hadn't understood what he meant. And Joddard had pushed him to go to art college, and from there he'd got on the Royal College Film Course and from there... Well, here. And that image had always been ticking away in the back of his head.

He'd used the big car move, as he called it, in his first music video. He'd insisted on it: the band didn't understand but lots of people liked the vid, and he got more work, then some commercials. Life was good, the future bright. And then Kate came by.

Kate had written this screenplay about a girl who'd drowned in light. That was the way she put it, and it only started to make sense the third time he read the thing. Very urban, very dark in places, but with a kind of humour all the way through. It was the ending that was the problem, the drowning bit: not a real drowning, but a psychic one. And then he'd realised. The white-out would do it. Kate had seen it differently, like she had her own agenda for it. No, blot her out with light, he'd said, and explained the idea. They'd argued most of an evening about it: ended up as lovers, though. So he'd borrowed some friends and some equipment and made a trailer for it, including the white-out. (Actually, he'd made it to see if the white-out worked.)

Channel 4 had found it really cool, and Arte liked it, too, and they'd somehow got the rest of the money. And made the film. During which he'd realised that Kate saw herself as the drowning girl: wanted the film made to sort out some deep hurts inside her, and that when the film was done she would be as well. He'd made the mistake of telling her about where the white-out shot came from. She hadn't liked that, and told him he hadn't understood. And however much he said he was beginning to understand, the more she moved away. It was, he thought, like the type on two pages of a book moving to the outside margins, until there was just this blank space between them. The day he showed her the final cut, she went.

The critics had liked the film, and it ran well for a few months, and there was talk of 'another revival of young British cinema and new talent,' and new projects: lots of scripts, discussions, offers, and more video work than he almost wanted. But he felt he was carrying this Kate sized white space around inside him all the time, which other lovers and other projects didn't fill: some mornings he felt as old as the wrinklies in that documentary. And tonight there was this award ceremony or whatever, for the film. And he kind of hoped there'd be the red carpet and the velvet ropes, but he'd heard they'd got some designer in to do the job. And as for Kate in the Cadillac…

each other. Mumbles are exchanged
'who's idea was this?'
Isn't that what's hi
from the telly?
Raymond rings the concierge bell for attention...The bell echoes...
turns to the sound of tinkling glass....
::::A thought: A good one! Had he a
First Woman
Who the hell's in charge here?
Raymond smiles back nervously at first....A thought. A good one! Had he a
moustache he would twirl it.
Will you stop sulking?
Veronique (cont'd)
(wearily, glaring at Jacques)
Fais un efffort quand meme.
She can't get out.
A man's boots step out from the garage porter cabin and start
to approach

'who's idea was this?'
name
Veronique
Fais voir. (She peers closer) Non, mais
la, tu as un bout de....Bouge pas.
....car wheels drive over the long rubber lead crossing the garage forecourt.
20. Ext. Forecourt of garage
Day
They exit the garage and
drive out onto the street
- the third woman snoring contently
against the back window.
We see
everything from the p.o.v.
Veronique
Fais voir. (She peers closer) Non, mais
la, tu as un bout de....Bouge pas.
....too much weight and shopping in the car, no room to find the handle.
back, panics, her glasses drop off.

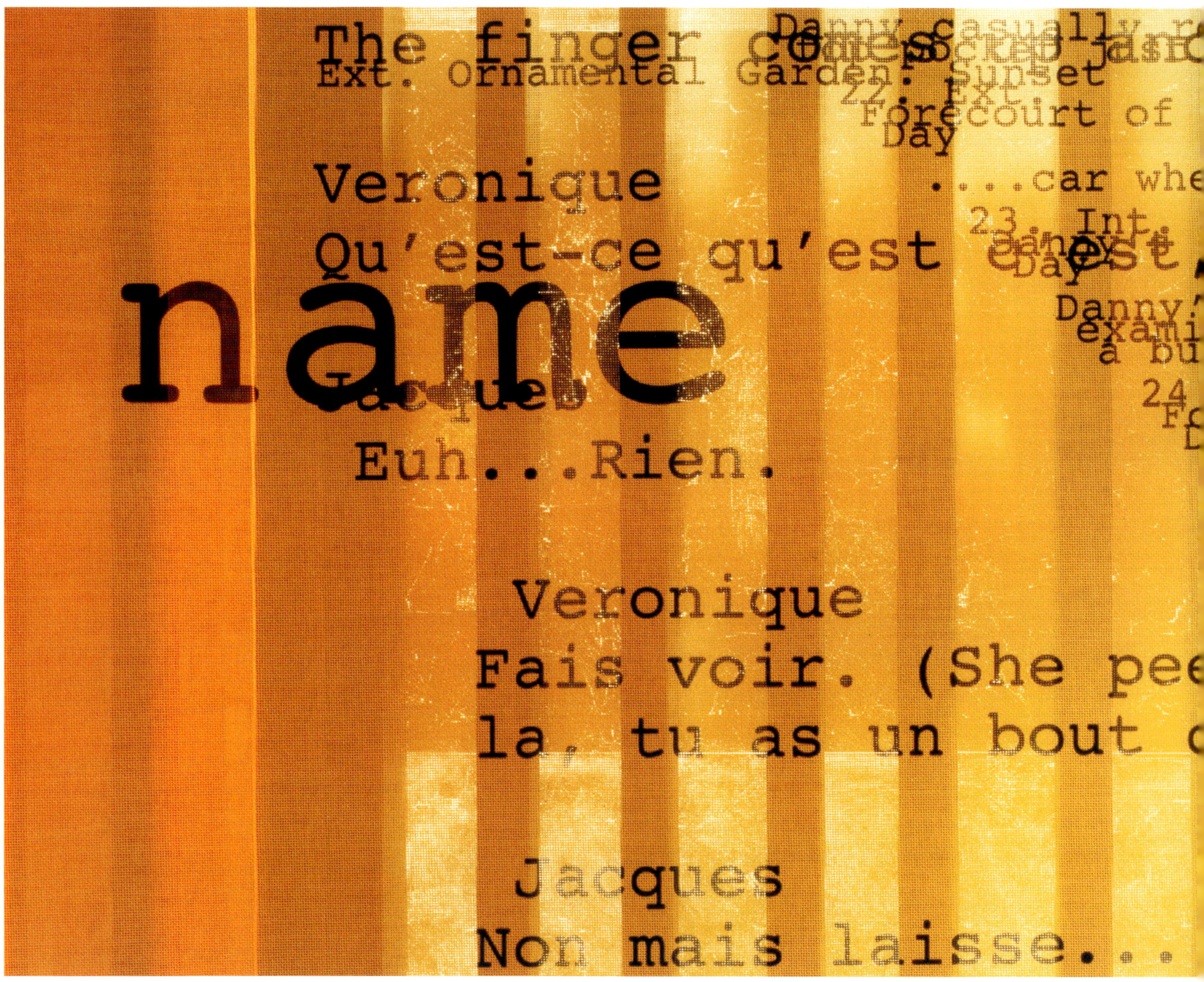
The finger
Ext. Ornamental Garden: Sunset
Forecourt of
Day
Veronique
....car whe
Qu'est-ce qu'est
name
Jacques
Euh...Rien.
Veronique
Fais voir. (She pee
la, tu as un bout
Jacques
Non mais laisse...

s up the money and places it in his
dabs at it leaving a smear.

rage

s drive over the long rubber lead crossing the ga

t cabin
la?

buzzer goes off. He steps up close to his CCTV ca
ng the new arrival, puffing on a fag before choos
on next to the monitor.

xt.
court of garage

s closer) Non, mais . . . . .
....Bouge pas.

3. Int/ Ext. Women's car / city street
...squeezed inside, the door's slammed closed.
The car twists and turns around - finding the
Mumbles are exchanged and aggravations aired 'never again' /
The women hate it - especially each other. Mumbles are exchanged
and aggravations aired 'never
again' /
'who's idea was this?'
Day
EVIL
Will
Int. Hotel Lobby. Dawn
Raymond rings the concierge bell for attention...The bell echoes...
turns to the sound of tinkling glass....

...........A thought. A good one! Had he a
First Woman.......
Who the hell's in charge here?
Who the hell's in charge here?
Raymond smiled back nervously at ......A thought. A good one! Had he a moustache he would twirl it.
She can't
Subtitle: Will you stop sulking?
Veronique (cont'd)
wearily, glaring at Jacques)
Fais un effort quand meme.
She can't get out.
ou stop sulking?
A man's boots step out from the garage porter cabin and start
......to approach
.... again'
DEVIL
RE

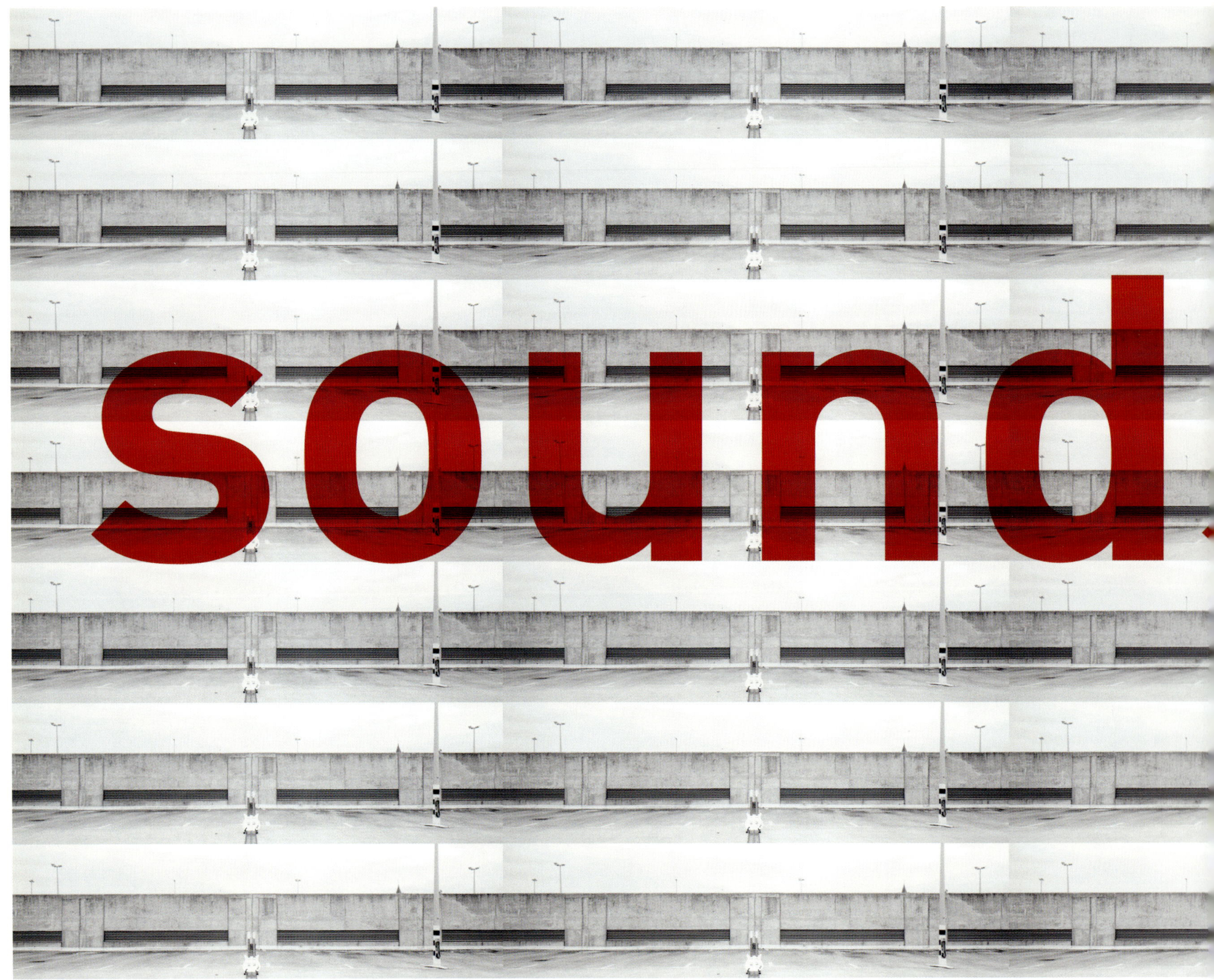
sound

scapes

REMEMBR

Dear Students of Film/Music Studies 407
Term Paper Assignment
Outline

We have been looking this term at the role of sound and music in classic Japanese film. For example, in Kurosawa's Throne of Blood at the use of chanting during the opening sequences to convey a sense of tragedy, through the fading hoofbeats that lead from the ride through the forest into the encounter with the sorceress, until the final moment when the sound of arrows hitting the wooden walls of the castle finally ceases, underscoring the usurper's death.

We also considered Tokyo Story, in particular the different levels of background sound between the urban and rural scenes, and the ways in which urban sound (traffic noise, sirens, etc.) could be perceived as 'modern' in contrast to the 'traditional' and more muted sounds of the countryside.

Returning to Kurosawa, we looked at how in the Seven Samurai the sounds of fighting and battle established historical and social differences: the samurai – already a doomed warrior elite – exercising their skills in silence – and recalling their combats in a quiet, almost remorseful way, while the armed peasants shouted and screamed to give themselves courage, and celebrated their victories with equal enthusiasm and fervour. The bandits are as well signalled out by their possession of firearms, and their use of these arms punctuates the audible and visual action of the story. Note here that the warriorclass had traditionally refused gunpowder (see reading notes). So sound effects separate the different social groups in the film, just as at the end the 'farmer turned samurai' returns to the rice field and joins in the planting song, while the two remaining samurai leave in silence. We contrasted these uses of sounds as social or cultural identifiers, or as heralds of changes in the action, with the use of sound in American films (particularly Westerns) of the same period, where sound and music is used in a much more narrative fashion (even if social groups are identified by sound cues: Indian drums for the war party, pianola for the saloon, bugles for the cavalry etc.)

From this basis, the final part of this study will concentrate on one specific film, Shimitzu's 1940s production Utajo Oboegaki, the story of an itinerant samishen player.

Background: the film tells, in a documentary fashion, the life of a blind player of the samishen who ekes out a living playing in inns and local theatres in northern Japan. While his life remains rooted in the traditions of his music, the events of the wider world – including the militarism that leads to the Second World War – thereby passes him by.

The Samishen: this is a traditional instrument, a kind of three-stringed fretless guitar, used as a folk instrument and in the popular theatre (though not to accompany Noh plays or other 'serious' drama.) It originated in Northern Japan, and is notoriously difficult to play, since the silk strings (that are plucked rather than fretted) lose their tuning within a few seconds. The player therefore has to tune the instrument continuously while playing it. (For background on this see the story 'Umugata and her servant' in the reading list, and Prof. Nogatura's essay on the samishen in the Dictionary of Japanese Music).

Context: the film clearly raises issues about the survival of traditional Japanese culture after the War, without being confrontational: the main character's blindness has the effect of absolving him from knowledge of both what Japan did and what happened to Japan, for example. There is a distinction here with the other films we have studied, which either are set deliberately in a distant past (though using a European story as motif in Throne of Blood) or choosing a moment of change (the ending of warrior culture in Seven Samurai). On the concept of Japanese culture as opposed to Western culture you should consider Tanizaki's pre-war essay In Praise of Shadows.

Your term paper should analyses these and other wider issues in the film, but concentrate particularly on the way the music of the samishen itself is used, the genre of the locations chosen and what they say about the social roles of the player, his audience and contemporary history. Of particular importance is the use of rural settings, whether villages, cultivated fields or wild country, (is the samishen primarily a rural or an urban instrument, for example) and the placing of incidental music, sound and sound levels. The main question that you may wish to answer is 'can a music instrument in itself animate, explain or accommodate a landscape?'

PlayStation®
in question
the HUMAN
I've NEVER been
HUMAN ENDEAVOUR
What bugs me about
Let me tell you

'Yes, you must go to the city during the dreams.' The man in the tourist office had said, or that is what it sounded like (his English was as bad as my Italian, but he was a pleasant chap.) The tourist office didn't get much business, I felt, though I had been in a couple of times, and always talked to Alessandro. This time he had suggested we take a glass of wine in the café next door, rather than discussing things over his desk. I concurred: we had sat at a table in the small piazza, and chatted about my travels and my studies. I suggested I should visit Siena, and he agreed with the idea. 'What about seeing the Palio?' I asked; it was a team horse-race in mediaeval costume around the main square, and a major tourist event. Alessandro nodded – was that what he meant by the dreams, perhaps – and thought for a moment. 'We will ask Antonio.' He waved to a man who was just crossing the square.

Antonio was the son of the local pharmacist, and supposedly managed one of the three chemist's shop his father owned. In fact he spent as little time there as possible, preferring a lethargic social life in the winter and the zealous seduction of visiting American and English students on monthly language courses in the summer. I knew this because his current girlfriend, Patricia, was a friend of mine, and Antonio, whom she found vastly entertaining, had candidly explained his lifestyle to her on their first date. I had indeed met Antonio once before, with Patricia. Coming over and greeting us, he at once dismissed the idea of tickets for the Palio as vulgar nonsense. He had a better plan. His father had cousins of some sort in Siena who had invited him to attend the Palio, and indeed bring a friend. Would I honour him and his family with my presence. I was astonished, wondering why he was not taking Patricia, but accepted at once. Fine: he would collect me early on the morning of the event – it was about an hour's drive – and we would make a day of it. Did I, by any chance, own a suit? Not that he, of course minded, but his relatives were a little old fashioned. I did not, but I did have a blazer in the colours of my old school, which I had kept as an awful reminder. That would do excellently, Antonio agreed.

Antonio's white Alfa Giulia was outside my door as promised. 'Ah! The jacket of honour!' he joked as he opened the passenger door: the colours, magenta, black and white, were poor in any light, and garish in Italian sunshine. As we set off I wondered again why he had chosen to invite an long-haired eighteen year old Englishman whom he hardly knew to such an event. As if guessing my thoughts, he explained, in an offhand way, that there was some sort of informal arrangement that he would in due course have to marry the daughter of these cousins. A family decision, of course, so bringing Patricia would have been inappropriate. I tried in halting Italian to show that I understood this delicacy of feeling, and the importance of family.

The Sienese family was indeed an important one: their house turned out to be a palazzo on the main square with a large balcony. We were introduced to them in a large and beautiful room on the first floor – I understood then why the Italians called it the piano nobile. If they were astonished at the guest Antonio had brought, they were far too polite to show it, and Antonio passed off the ghastly blazer as the insignia of a famous school and the bearer as an honours student of jurisprudence at the University of Oxford, which they took as a mark of gentility and eccentricity in equal proportions. I was even introduced to the fiancée, Beatrice, as well as her parents and grandparents, various aunts and uncles, and a dozen cousins. Beatrice's father, Bernardo, spoke good English, which he cheerfully explained he had learned as a prisoner-of-war in Canada 'during Mussolini's stupid war in Libya.' He candidly explained that he had been drafted, pushed into becoming an officer, and was very proud that none of his men were killed in action before he was captured. He offered to explain the Palio to me, as we went out onto the balcony after the extensive and excellent lunch.

Bernardo told me about the contrade, the neighbourhood companies that competed, and the complex pacts, negotiations, bets and bribes that went on between them. He detailed the traditions and emblems of the corteo storico, the parade that precedes the final race, as each appeared. ('But I think,' he added in a whisper, 'that it was all invented by Mussolini and the Church, as a game to please the people.') The pageantry and the flag-waving were elegant and vigorous, but what animated the scene was the crowd in the Piazza del Campo itself. The spectators were thrilled and passionate, cheering their teams and booing their opponents, applauding the flag-bearers. If it was a game, they were engrossed in it, all of them, children and parents, locals and tourists. Looking at them I felt I shared, at a distance, their excitements, their hopes, their fears. The final race only lasted a couple of minutes, but from the faces of the crowd they wanted it to go on forever. Was that what Alessandro meant by going there during the dreams?

On the way home Antonio was quiet and subdued. Had I liked Beatrice? I had found her molto gentile. And her father? A wonderful man, such a fine host. Had my parents decided whom I would marry? No, not yet (and not ever, if I had any choice.) And after university, would I work with my father? No, I would probably go to London. 'Ah, amico mio,' he said, 'if only I had your life and my dreams. What a game it would be!'

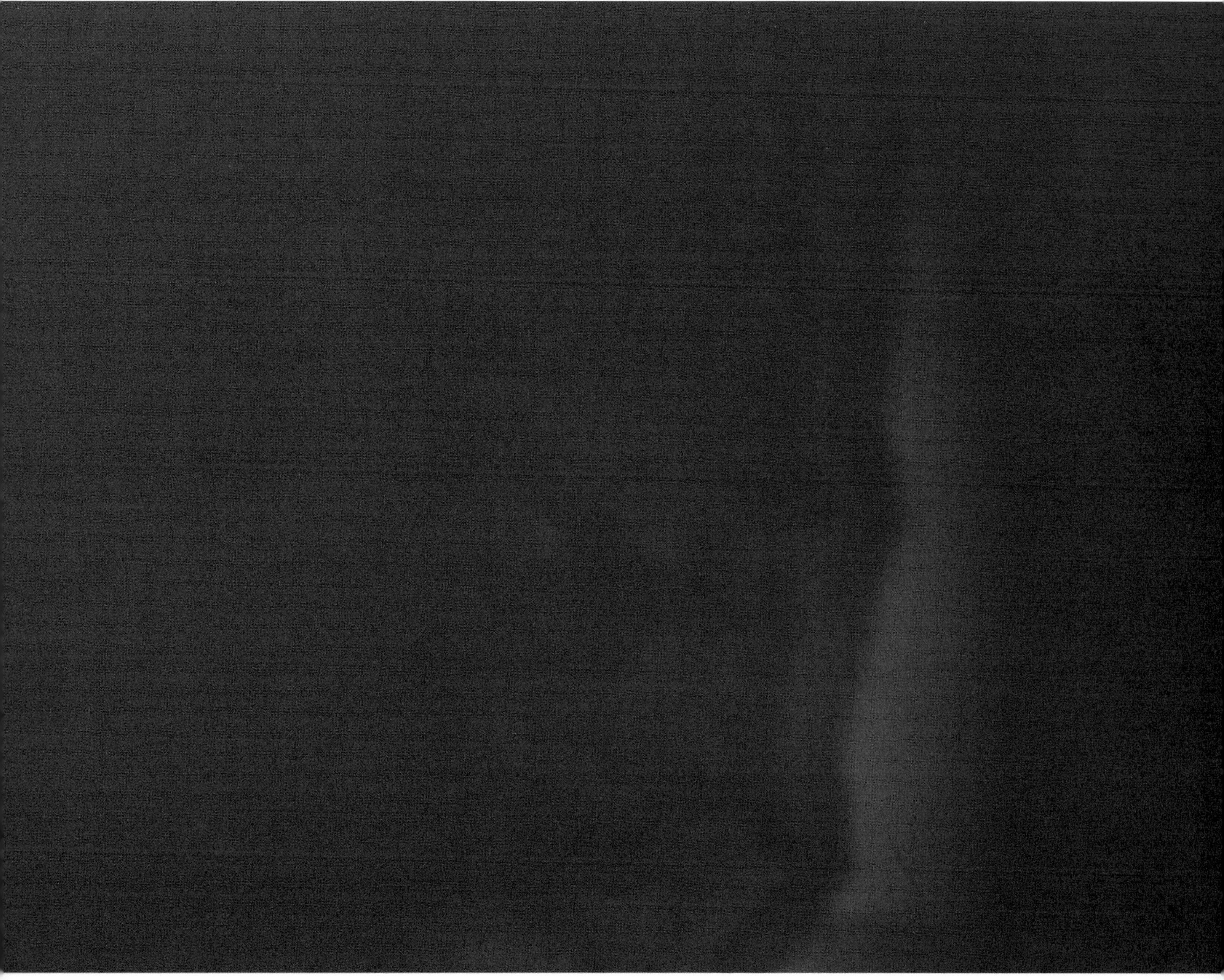

wip3out
formula one '99
this is football
tarzan
PlayStation
PlayStation
PlayStation

PlayStation

SONY

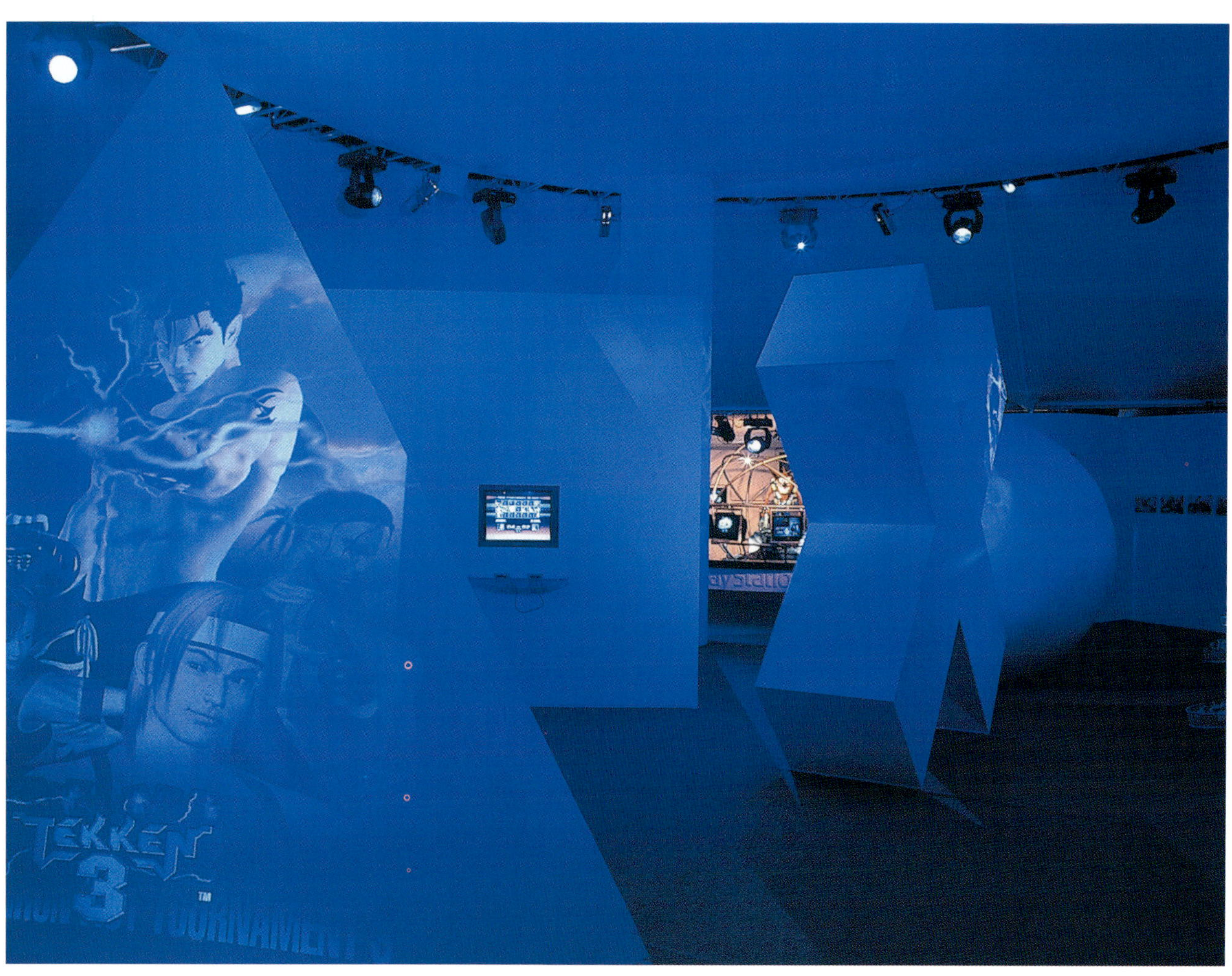
TEKKEN
3
TM

**“let me tell you what bugs me about human endeavour.
i’ve never been the human in question.
have you...?
mankind went to the moon.
i don’t even know where grimsby is.
fuck progress by proxy.**

**it's time for diy of the mind...
land on your own moon.
it's no longer about what they can achieve
out there on your behalf.
but what we can experience up here
in our own time.
it's called mental wealth.
spend. spend. spend."**

'Mental Wealth' poem used as vinyl type on the floor of the exhibition

one, numero uno worldwide

*1*1*1

, 0 0 0, 1

GERMANY

we love you virgin
Virgin Interactive Entertainment 19
Virgin Interactive Entertainment
El número uno.
SPAIN IS VERY HOT

Nummer Eins
Nummer Eins
Germany cut out the competition

The grass is greener in the UK
not
number one

She had always wanted to travel: no, that's not right. She had always dreamed of travelling, and wanted to dream of travelling. But the few times she had actually travelled, she hadn't really liked it. As a schoolgirl she had been on a train trip to London; at eight years old she's been really excited about the train ride, but no-one had told her the train moved like that, and she'd had an awful shock, and some of the boys in her class had laughed at her, called her Sissy Chrissy. She'd flown to Spain once, on a package with some teenage friends. But everyone there had seemed to be from Manchester, and they all drank too much, and someone had spilt red wine on her new white dress. She'd bought a stuffed toy of a Spanish donkey as a present for her nephew, but had to check it into the hold and missed it at the airport on the way home. She sometimes imagined it going round and round on the luggage ramp at Luton airport, lost like Paddington Bear at the station but not so much fun…

So Chrissy read romances about travel, and watched films set in foreign cities, and looked at travel magazines and imagined herself on those beaches or in those bars. She and her best friend Sally would go and have a drink after work, and talk about all the places they would travel to, one day. And the men they might meet: American or Spanish, Italian or French. And the fun they might have and the things they might do: every week they'd have a 'bit of plot and giggle,' as Sally put it, dreaming up even more outrageous things to do in even more outlandish places. The twin Russian snowboard champions ('always ends in ski!' they'd chorused.) Or the Andalusian ballet dancers ('look, no andas!') Or those bungee jumping instructors in Cuba: 'taut but elastic' Chrissy had said – 'and who taught them that but us!' Sally had replied; they still laughed over that.

They never went anywhere, in the end: not enough time, not enough money after clothes and clubbing. Until one day Sally went and met Charles, and now she only wanted to talk about where they were going on the honeymoon – Florida as of last Friday, Tunisia the week before. And somehow the talk wasn't as fun any more. Oh, Chrissy was going to be a bridesmaid, the chief bridesmaid no less, and she loved discussing the plans for the clothes and the reception and who was coming. It was Sally's big day, and Chrissy was happy for her, even imagining, selflessly, Sally and Charles in some of her favourite situations. But somehow these real people and real events weren't as exciting as what there had been before. Then travel had been larger than life, foreign had been exotic.

Then Charles had mentioned that the best man was coming over from Boston. Wowee! What had that airline hostess she'd met once said? 'The captain used to say to the passengers landing at Boston 'Welcome to Boston, the Athens of the North and the hub of the Universe'.' What was he like, she asked Charles, and what did he do. 'A tall guy called John,' Charles had said,' who teaches computing or something.' That was a good sign: wasn't Harvard in Boston, or Yale or MIT or something. And tall, too. Maybe not as tall as the Texan in Four Weddings and a Funeral, perhaps, but still an omen, of a sort. A real American: and just for her, as chief bridesmaid and best man, well, you knew what everyone said…

The wedding day came, and John too. He was tall, with fair hair and large blue eyes: quite good looking, quite relaxed. She'd been introduced to him briefly before the wedding: he'd said 'Hi' and shaken hands with a smile, a nice smile. His accent wasn't very American, she thought fleetingly. Waiting for the guests at the reception he had been at the other end of the line from her, but she found they were sitting next to each other at table. He was charming, asking her how long she had known Charles and Sally, what her job was, who else she knew at the party. Politely not saying much about himself. Finally she asked him directly: 'are you from Boston?' 'I work there,' he said, 'for the moment. I like the countryside there, but the middle of Lincolnshire is not exactly fun.' Lincolnshire, she thought. Oh no! The other Boston, the one here. What had Raymond Chandler once said: 'I guess God made Boston on a wet Sunday.' She felt utterly dejected, and an utter fool. But only for a moment, for John was still speaking. 'Yes, it's nice here, but I can't wait to get back to Seattle.' Seattle, now that was sleepless.

virgin
we love you
i love you

big,
turnover
bigger
bigg
biggest
turnover

VIE is part of a
group with a market capital estim

you're number one

we love you

now that's what I call a lot of zeros!

$25

zero

zero

zero

zero

zero

zero

zero

bi

turnover
biggest

Scuz was a focus groupie: that's what he'd always told them. 'Look,' he'd go, ' that supermarket is selling aromatherapy washing up liquid. So! I was the guy who told the focus group that housewives worried about their dishes. I mean, I didn't mean worried about their dishes happiness, just the cleanliness bit, but this guy from the management got real excited, and so when I said, hey! aromatherapy they really went for it.' Ros and Suzi didn't really believe Scuz. They thought he spent all his time behind his computer or gameplay screen and didn't interact with the real world at all. So who would want to know his opinions, let alone pay him for them. Mind you, he'd been right about the Burgundy flavoured crisps. But not about the Boy Scout motifs on the trainers. Nor the beer pump, but that wasn't surprising, the way he told it.

'You see,' Scuz had said, 'the agency wanted ideas a beer to sell in Indian restaurants. So they asked me and about half a dozen guys they'd found someplace. The others were really laddish: studs and tattoos and ten pints of lager. Not very nice at all, and very, very racist: who knows how the guys at the marketing company found them. One, shaven headed and really rough, was quite upset when he found out it was beer for Indians, threatened to walk out. But the guy from the agency calmed him down: it wasn't for Indians, but for customers in their restaurants. So we talked about all sorts of things, until finally one guy, who hadn't said much but who looked as if he was thinking hard, suddenly put up his hand, like he was back in class. "I know, I know," he said, "have a little figure of Hitler on the bar, saluting, like, and when you pull his arm down the beer could come out of his mouth." He looked inspired, as if he'd just decoded the human genome and shot the winning goal in the World Cup at the same time. The guy from the agency looked as if he'd been hit with a brick. I was trying so hard not to laugh, 'cos the guy wouldn't have thought it funny. It was wonderful, really. I can't remember what we decided after that, at all.'

Roz and Suzie would drop in on Scuz most Fridays and Saturdays before going out to the club: he was always so calm and quiet, but with some story for them, either off the Internet or from this odd work he seemed to do. He was always there, always awake, with his computer screen often the only light in the room.They'd sometimes come back to his place after the club, if they'd not hooked up with anyone there: he never seemed to sleep, and would offer them wine or breakfast, a bed to sleep in or a shoulder to cry on or just someone to share a joke or a joint with. And they liked his stories, even the one about Hitler, which they half-believed, having met some odd types in their time. But the new story: never.

According to Scuz, he'd been walking near the motorway bridge the other afternoon when he'd noticed really bright lights and strange people underneath it. 'Yea. aliens,' said Roz. 'Again' said Suzie,'no taste, those aliens.' No, said Scuz, it was a photographic shoot. 'There was this girl, really something, crawling all over a Ford Cortina.' 'Cortina!' the girls shrieked. 'Not just any old Cortina,' Scuz explained seriously, 'a Lotus Cortina, with those fat poggy tyres. That's what made it so cool.' 'So it was a car shoot, or fashion, or what?' Roz asked. 'I got talking to one of the guys,' Scuz explained, 'and he said it was for an ad for a new game console. He said they were targeting the young female market. You know, girls playing computer games. He showed me the machine. Pretty neat, I thought.'

And that did it. Alien abduction, yes, Hitler beer pumps, even. But girls playing computer games! No way. Roz and Suzie knew that. But they liked Scuz and his stories.

SUNDAY MORNING 02:43

SUNDAY EVENING 21:00

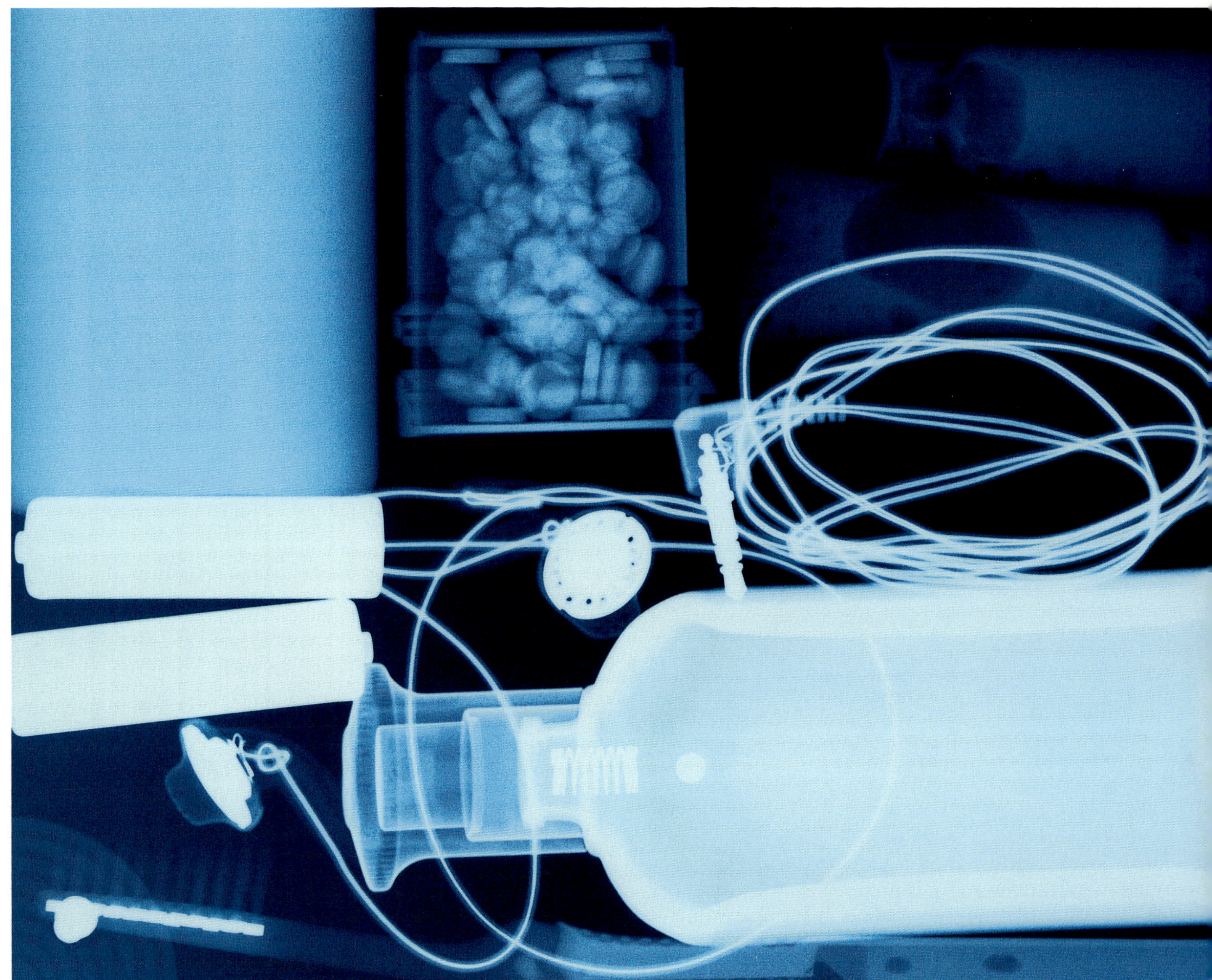

HEATHROW AIRPORT 16:42

SATURDAY MORNING 02:15
get some colour on your cheeks.
40 hours continuous playtime. 18 hot titles. 16bit colour power. 6 cool cases. 1 machine. Zero alternative.
SNK
NeoGeo £59.99 Games £24.99. Available at Electronics Boutique, Game, HMV, MVC, Dixons, Currys, @Jakarta, Beatties and all good independent retailers.

SUNDAY EVENING 21:00
get some time together.
40 hours continuous playtime. 18 hot titles. 16bit colour power. 6 cool cases. 1 machine. Zero alternative.
SNK.
NeoGeo £59.99 Games £24.99. Available at Electronics Boutique, Game, HMV, MVC, Dixons, Currys, @Jakarta, Beatties and all good independent retailers.

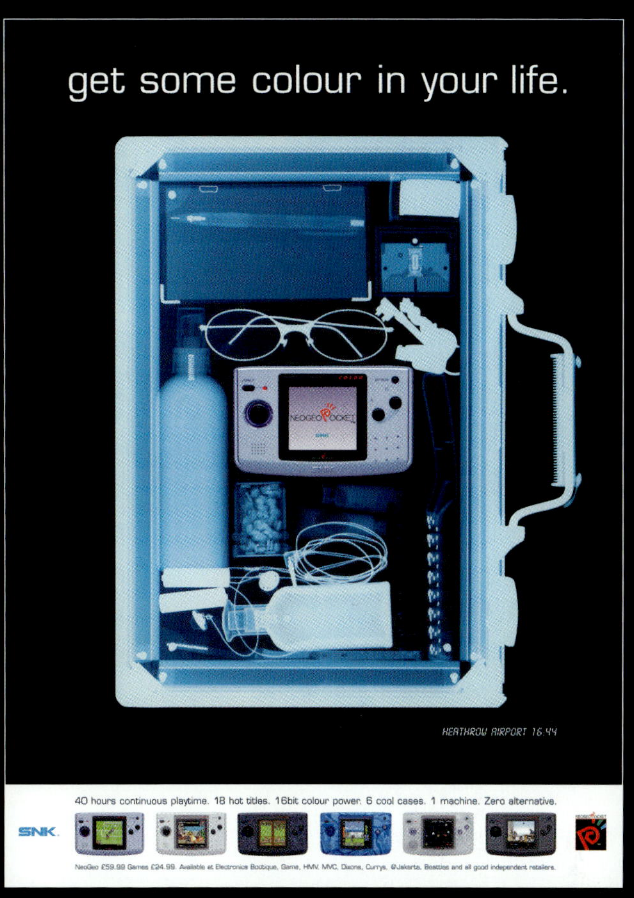
get some colour in your life.
HEATHROW AIRPORT 16:44
40 hours continuous playtime. 18 hot titles. 16bit colour power. 6 cool cases. 1 machine. Zero alternative.
SNK.
NeoGeo £59.99 Games £24.99. Available at Electronics Boutique, Game, HMV, MVC, Dixons, Currys, @Jakarta, Beatties and all good independent retailers.

Tim Rich, at the time editor of Graphics International, first suggested I took a look at Martin Root's work. He showed me an image of a small trade fair stand project the company had done some time ago: a circular wall of shimmering silver drapes encasing a glitterball in the ceiling, and around the walls, a row of simple white computer stands (the project was for a presentation interior for a computer games company) each surmounted by a white neon halo. It was very simple and very effective.

When I got to see Root Design Associates, a fortuitous misunderstanding occurred. Martin had prepared for me, not his work at the 1995 ECTS fair, but a more recent project for the same show in 1996. This was a much larger stand for Virgin Interactive Entertainment. What I saw was Chartres Cathedral on acid, or a nightmare from the Name of the Rose. A monastery for a strange cult indeed: corner towers surmounted by monstrous gargoyles on the outside of the two-level structure, in the crypt (at ground level, but only accessible from the upper floor) a vivarium for the resident snake and a well surmounted by a Star of David grille, attended by monks in red and black robes, probably chanting canticles for Liebowitz.

Computer games show stands containing mock-mediaeval imagery are not uncommon, given the dungeon and dragonish nature of many games, and the odd helmeted axeman or club-bearing nomad in a fur loincloth could be found, carefully cut out of heavy card and stood upright, outside many stands. But those examples are normally taken directly from the games they are promoting. What I was seeing here was nothing less than a complete identity – called the Virgin Brotherhood – created solely for this event, and in its own space, with a wealth of detail down to lettered banners in the entrance hall and the quincunx cover on the press pack. It all suggested an enthusiastic and creative imagination at work together with an ability to think in three dimensions and beyond the conventions of a brief. And a great sense of fun, as well. Looking back at this project over five years of root's work, both in exhibition design and other graphics, it seems in many ways very different in style and approach from the work Martin and his colleagues are doing today. Yet with hindsight there are parallels: the design and theming was indeed bold and expressive, but the flamboyance was handled with a certain restraint. The exterior, for all its wild imagery, was almost monochrome, so heightening the visitors' experience of the rich reds and golds within. The same control and balance shows through in the current work. And the sense of completeness that was there: the depth of detail that made the Virgin confection convincing runs still into the handling of very different and equally complex projects now.

Martin today describes his work as 'much more minimal.' It is true that some reduction has been going on: the company name has been pared back from Root Design Associates Limited to Root Design, then to root., and now to root, for example. Their studio is on the east of the City of London, near the old Spitalfields market, on the top floor in a quiet side-street. Martin's own office, which looks out westwards over a pattern of roofs, at one time contained a desk, meeting table and upright chairs. A couple of years later the table and chairs had gone in favour of armchairs and a coffee table, while an i-Mac occupied the desk. Today the desk is half the size, with enough space for Martin's i-Book. Martin's small team are in the main part of the studio, in a familiar clutter of large screens and Mac G4s, while a large flatscreen television by the reception desk is hardwired to MTV. The atmosphere is informal, the colours pale. Not minimal as much as cool.

What Martin has achieved over recent years is not the normal ascetic, reductive minimalism found in some contemporary architecture or in conceptual art. Rather he has refined the design process and his design solutions to work with a smaller and smaller array of elements, each one chosen to maximise its individual impact, and often developed from a single rather than a multiple concept.

One feature of many root graphic projects is their use of photography. Not stock photography digitally improved on the screen, but original work from high profile photographers such as Simon Emmett, Sandrine Dulermo, Lee Strickland and Tom Dunkley. For example, when root were asked to work on the campaign for the band Soundproof, they asked Kai Weichman to shoot the photography, and for the Soundscapes brochure they turned to Kevin Griffin. Working with people of this calibre requires both judgement and confidence if the partnership is to be a creative one. It is evidence of how root have extended the boundaries of the designer's role, moving into creating advertising campaigns, as with SNK, and into directing videos for bands and musicians such as Mis-teeq, Wamdue Project and McAlmont. Here their work has been characterised by the same sparseness and acuity to be found in their graphics and trade fair design.

For a design company that works so much with the music business, where bright lights and loud noises are the norm, such minimalism might seem an unusual approach. That it is the right one, however, is not in doubt. Among their clients is the Irish boy-band Westlife. root have been responsible for their graphic image from the start of their record-breaking career, designing their identity, the covers for their singles and CDs, and art-directing much of their photography. By reducing the graphic decoration to a minimum, the images of the five singers dominated the whole. 'Minimum', however, does not mean unplanned or unsubtle. In the music industry the positioning of a new band in a complex and shifting market is a question of key importance, and the visual element therein a major factor. root's approach is to analyse this positioning and devise the appropriate solution, not to apply a house style or formula (the different ways in which Westlife and Vega4, for example, are treated is proof of this.) Minimalism is the result of analysis, not a precondition.

Areas such as computer games, pop music and trade fairs have often been seen as ancillary to the 'proper' business of design. A graphic designer's ideal portfolio should, in this view, be judged on signage, corporate identity, packaging and design for print. (For the record, root has worked in many of these fields: take their identity work for the public relations company OneVoice, for the Technology for Marketing event or for Business Golf Corporation, for example.) Today, however, the design agenda is often relevant to what could be termed the 'leisure takeover.' I use this term to suggest that products no longer stand alone in the marketplace, but are linked in their presentation and language to a wider and wider array of concepts and issues. This associative phenomenon, which now goes way beyond simple marketing strategies, is not new: what has been happening recently is that the focus of association has been moving through lifestyle more and more towards the models provided by the leisure and entertainment industry, and particularly the music business. It is this change that makes root's work so relevant.

Purists might argue that something as commercially driven and evanescent as pop music cannot be taken seriously as a cultural phenomenon. But that would involve ignoring the role of newspapers and magazines in the popular culture of the 19th century and rock and roll in the 20th – all enterprises that were and are wholly commercial. A mature view of design accepts that it operates, for the most part, in this environment, but that does not imply that design can be unprincipled. root bring to their work an organisational discipline and a sense of the contemporary aesthetic. Their work is not simply driven by the requirements of clients, but is informed by a sense of design values and social realities. In a complex and volatile market – for in the music industry change is the only constant – they deliver vision and excitement, relevance and sensuality.

Open
24 HOURS

Vega4 is a band which, unlike some of the new acts fabricated by record companies and television shows, writes and performs its own music. After a few years playing gigs in the UK and Europe, they were awarded a recording contract in 2001, and root won the creative pitch to design and develop an identity and campaign for them, and to use this on their single and album releases, due in 2002.

The CD fold-out is based on what appears to be a satellite image of a West Coast American suburb, with individual locations highlighted and linked to further images: the diner, the park bench, the pool. These images illustrate the connections people have at any given moment, encapsulating a snap shot of life.

The advantage of this approach, quite apart from its originality, is that it allows the individual personalities of the band members to emerge later, if required. The four band members are present, for example eating in the diner, and shot against the sun in the image used on the front cover, but they are hardly identifiable.

root are working on developing the campaign for Vega4, and are consulting on their stage shows. For Martin the advantage of working with the band from the beginning of their recording career is that it means their graphic personality evolves alongside their music, rather than being imposed on it from the outside or retro-fitted to an existing body of work.

The Specialists®

dat:

loc:

VIRGIN INTERACTIVE, PILLAR ROOM STAND, ECTS 2000

WARNING: OTHER STANDS MAY CAUSE DROWSINESS

* TO BE TAKEN DAILY - 03,04,05 SEPT 00 *

keep out of reach of children

Stands at trade fairs are today part of the mature corporate vocabulary, and so have to be consistent in their content and approach with the client's overall message. This does not mean that the only phraseology allowed has to come from the identity manual, however, particularly in the context of a trade fair that is primarily business to business. Here an established company can allow its message to be expressed in metaphor.

For Virgin Interactive at the ECTS show in 2000, root proposed a quasi-medical theme, under the title of 'The Specialists,' a subtle hint at the company's expertise in computer games. Sans-serif lettering on coloured bands imitated hospital signage systems, while the messages parodied healthcare warnings on medicines ('other stands may cause drowsiness.') The press packs were pill-boxes, the seating white and waiting-room formal, the drinks at the bar delivered from infusion bags.

To formulate a light-hearted design of this kind is not difficult: the challenge lies in carrying it through with sufficient control and detail for it to be convincing, and also not to conceal the real content of the stand – the new products and services the client is offering – behind the entertainment. In this case it is the structure of the design work that sustains the challenge.

tea's gone cold

'A singer who transcends any trends' was how the music press welcomed the singer-songwriter Dido's start of her solo career: hardly of her musical career as she was a classical musician before starting a vocal career. For her debut CD, No Angel, Cheeky records commissioned a set of television commercials from root (30, 20 and 10 seconds respectively.) The album went on to become the most popular album of the year on Billboard's 2001 chart.

At the heart of Dido's music is her lyrical flow and her engagement with vivid emotional issues. The designers needed to find an appropriate visual metaphor, and so they chose two devices. For the typography, they used a distressed extra-bold sans serif face, all in lowercase, and for the imagery a crisp jagged line that drew the outline of Dido's figure while following the rhythms of the two tracks used in the commercials, Thank You and Here With Me.

For root the transition from graphics to four-dimensional design was eased both by their experience in creating events around their trade-fair stands and through their website and video work. The integration of type and image may seem at first to be simply a graphic problem, but in fact to relate that to a timeframe and a score is a completely different question.

Dido thirty second television commercial

Int

'this scene was

Now

As ac e: sl p: a oo e ick u

grc

anc le e: ay ea ca: si e.

The fi e s ll d Bs at l le

Ext. Ornamenta árc et

ct ga e

Day

Veronique . ar eel drive over

Qu'est-ce qu'est que c'est, la?

name

Danny's buzzer goes

examining the

a button next to the

24. Ext.

Forecourt

Day

Jacques

Eun...Rien.

Veronique

Fais voir. (She peers closer) Non, mai

la tu as un bout de ...Bouge pas.

Jacques

Non mais ... .

His hand come up and plucks his eyeball

:: :: :: :: :: :: :: ::

Danny real en ladies?

Film awards such as the Oscar and Golden Globe ceremonies, are an important part in promoting the film business (and the business of film) as well as providing glamour and gossip to the media. Other film awards not only honour film-makers, but also promote film as a cultural activity. These can be just as important, if less star-studded. When the mobile phone company Orange decided to sponsor a masterclass with Mike Leigh, followed by their awards for new independent short films, they chose the National Film Theatre in London as the appropriate setting and invited root to create the interior environment for the event and the subsequent party.

For root, plush and paparazzi were not the answer: the event needed structure, not stars. Their solution was based on clips, stills and texts from the films being honoured and discussed. These were applied to wall-panels and to projection screens, while an overall orange tint marked out the sponsor. By moving from names to words and from titles to frames the emphasis of the event was subtly shifted towards a cultural and intellectual focus.

The brief called for the entrance and green room and stage to be decked out for the awards event, as was the 1920 bar in Clerkenwell where the party for film-makers was held after the event. By moving from wall panels to backlit screens to projections, the design solution generated a dynamic that helped draw the audience progressively into the excitement of the event.

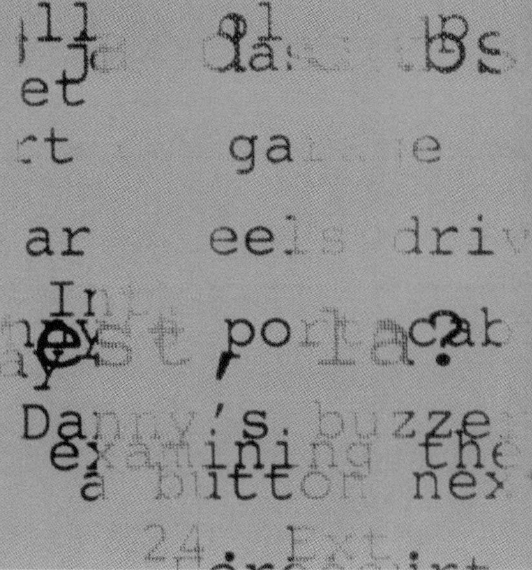

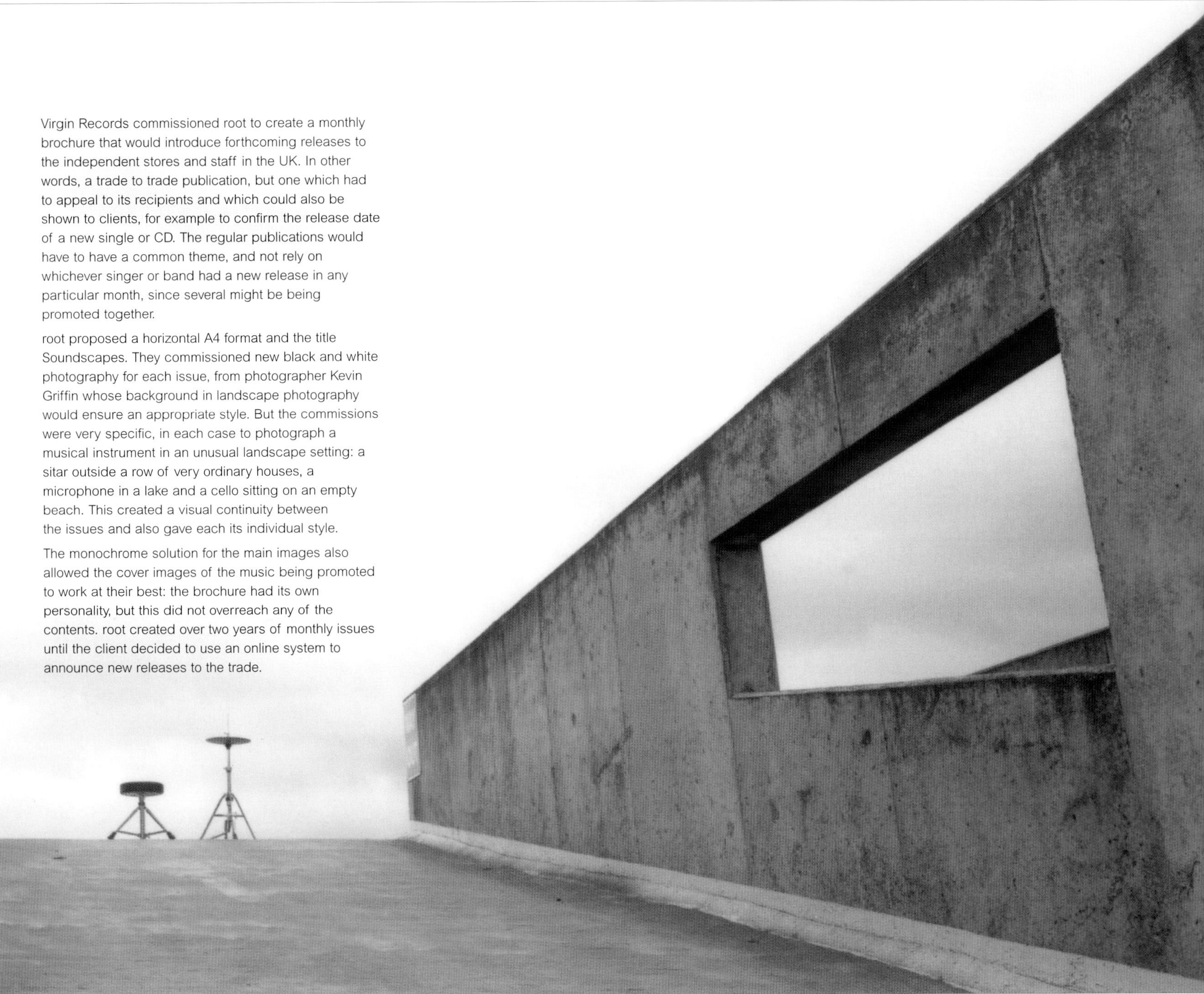

Virgin Records commissioned root to create a monthly brochure that would introduce forthcoming releases to the independent stores and staff in the UK. In other words, a trade to trade publication, but one which had to appeal to its recipients and which could also be shown to clients, for example to confirm the release date of a new single or CD. The regular publications would have to have a common theme, and not rely on whichever singer or band had a new release in any particular month, since several might be being promoted together.

root proposed a horizontal A4 format and the title Soundscapes. They commissioned new black and white photography for each issue, from photographer Kevin Griffin whose background in landscape photography would ensure an appropriate style. But the commissions were very specific, in each case to photograph a musical instrument in an unusual landscape setting: a sitar outside a row of very ordinary houses, a microphone in a lake and a cello sitting on an empty beach. This created a visual continuity between the issues and also gave each its individual style.

The monochrome solution for the main images also allowed the cover images of the music being promoted to work at their best: the brochure had its own personality, but this did not overreach any of the contents. root created over two years of monthly issues until the client decided to use an online system to announce new releases to the trade.

The computer games industry finds itself regularly between two conflicting pressures. On the one hand it knows that its customers expect excitement, thrills and spills from its products, and on the other it knows that there is a host of critics ready to accuse it of damaging or exploiting the same customers, on every level from the social to the moral to even the physical. The position to adopt in such a case could perhaps be described as responsible enthusiasm.

Translate this into a trade fair stand, as Sony PlayStation invited root to do at the 1999 ECTS show in London, and the result is a swing of emphasis. Instead of clamouring to present the characters or scenes of the new season's games, the stand suggests the social role of game-playing: something to be shared, something for all ages. The entrance to the stand is a low-lit passageway with a poem printed on the floor and regular images hung on the walls, like an officer foyer. The main space is lit evenly, with areas for individual products picked out in sober colours. But this understatement is at the same time forceful, as the images chosen are anything but anodyne: they are, in some ways, as dramatic as any scene from a computer game.

root's solution for Sony not only emphasised, as the brief required, the social aspect of computer gaming. It also quietly reinforced Sony's leading position in the market, saying, in effect, that Sony did not have to shout its wares from the housetops but could afford a more relaxed but equally committed position.

'It was a bit like an annual report,' Martin explains, 'though with more general financial information.' The Virgin Interactive brochure may be a business to business document of such a kind, but hardly looks like one. It is more a holiday guide for the demented: a parody of a tourist on an impossible beach, the chic-est catwalk poodle in decades… And following this gallery of improbable clients, a series of simple, bold statements made graphically but with an architectonic feel, as if a trade stand was built into the pages.

The images are digitally enhanced, to stress the effects of exaggeration and set on vivid colours, while more sober backgrounds are used for the 'information' pages. Here angled type in perspective patterns gives the three-dimensional effect that builds a solidity into the client's message, which is in turn set out in bold and direct statements. Hardly the genteel approach of the company report.

But the message is the right one. It says that here is a funky, unusual, active and positive company – interesting people to do business with: so come and join the party. The aim of the project was to find business partners in new markets worldwide, especially in America, and for this the choice of imagery is bold and subtle. The parodic and comic element is clear at first glance, but the images gain in depth and content on further study, suggesting that the company they describe is competent all the way through.

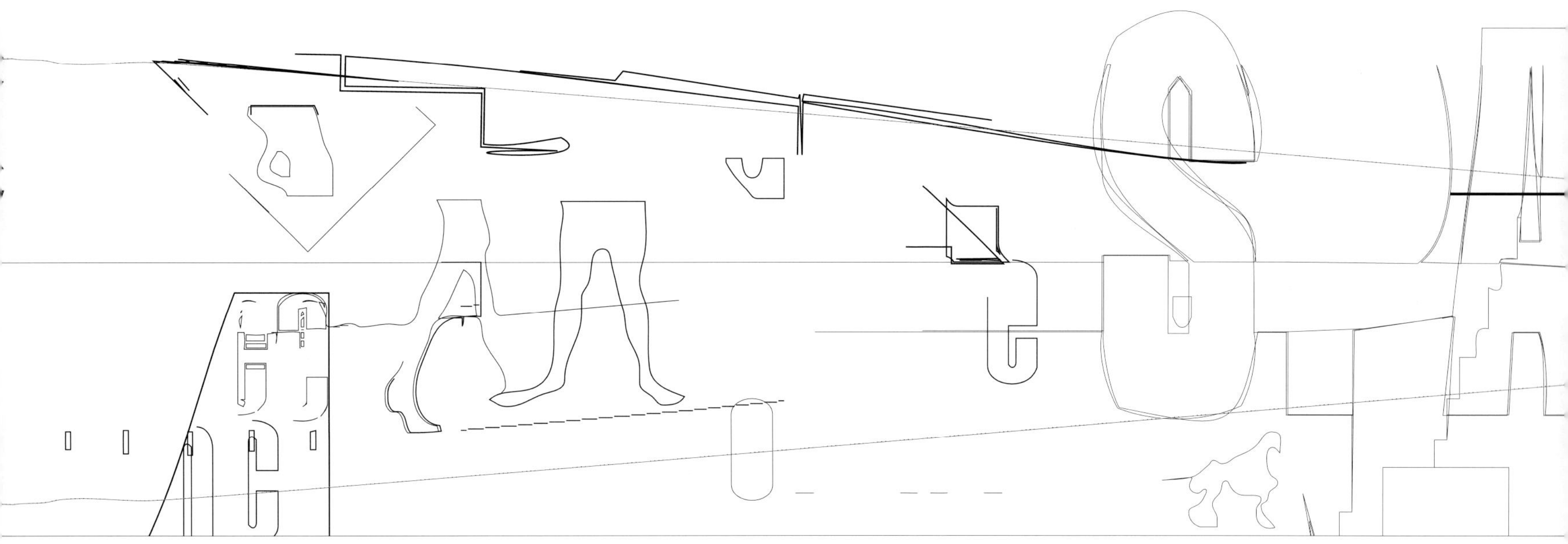

Normally an advertising agency appoints designers for a project – or uses an in-house team. When SNK launched their computer game machine in 2000, they asked root, who had worked on the packaging design, to create the advertising campaign, asking their advertising agency only to handle media space for the ads. The new machine, called the NeoGeo Pocket Colour, was intended to appeal to an older and more sophisticated market than the teenage and younger gamers targeted by Nintendo and Sony.

The advertisements were intended for three markets: general lifestyle magazines, men's magazines and business/travel magazines, and the message to each was slightly different, though the overall theme was consistent. Here was a grown-up toy, a neat and necessary lifestyle object: you and your partner could share a game in the evening, or you could pack it along on a business trip.

root used specially commissioned photography for the main body of the adverts, and a strapline that suggested a place and time, as well as a joking comment, sometimes literally cheeky. The simple sophistication of root's solution aligned it with the expectations of the product, itself, like the lifestyle magazines for men in which it was advertised, a crossover, a new generation of product that has moved from one market segment to another.

NO

The Oxfordshire-based group Medal won considerable acclaim for their first CD, Drop Your Weapon. The critics liked the mixture of standard pop with avant-garde musical treatments and direct and urban lyrics. The group subsequently decided to follow their own dreams, and moved from Polydor to their own label, El Producto. While at Polydor they had worked with root developing visual concepts to be used during their live performances in the UK and elsewhere.

'We found keywords from their lyrics,' Martin explains, 'and visualised them in very direct ways, as if they were signs and symbols in an urban landscape.' The images which picked up on the distinctive lyrics were back-projected, at low resolution, onto the stage set and also directly over the band.

COLD T

Advertisement for BMG records

Stills from Wamdue Project music promo

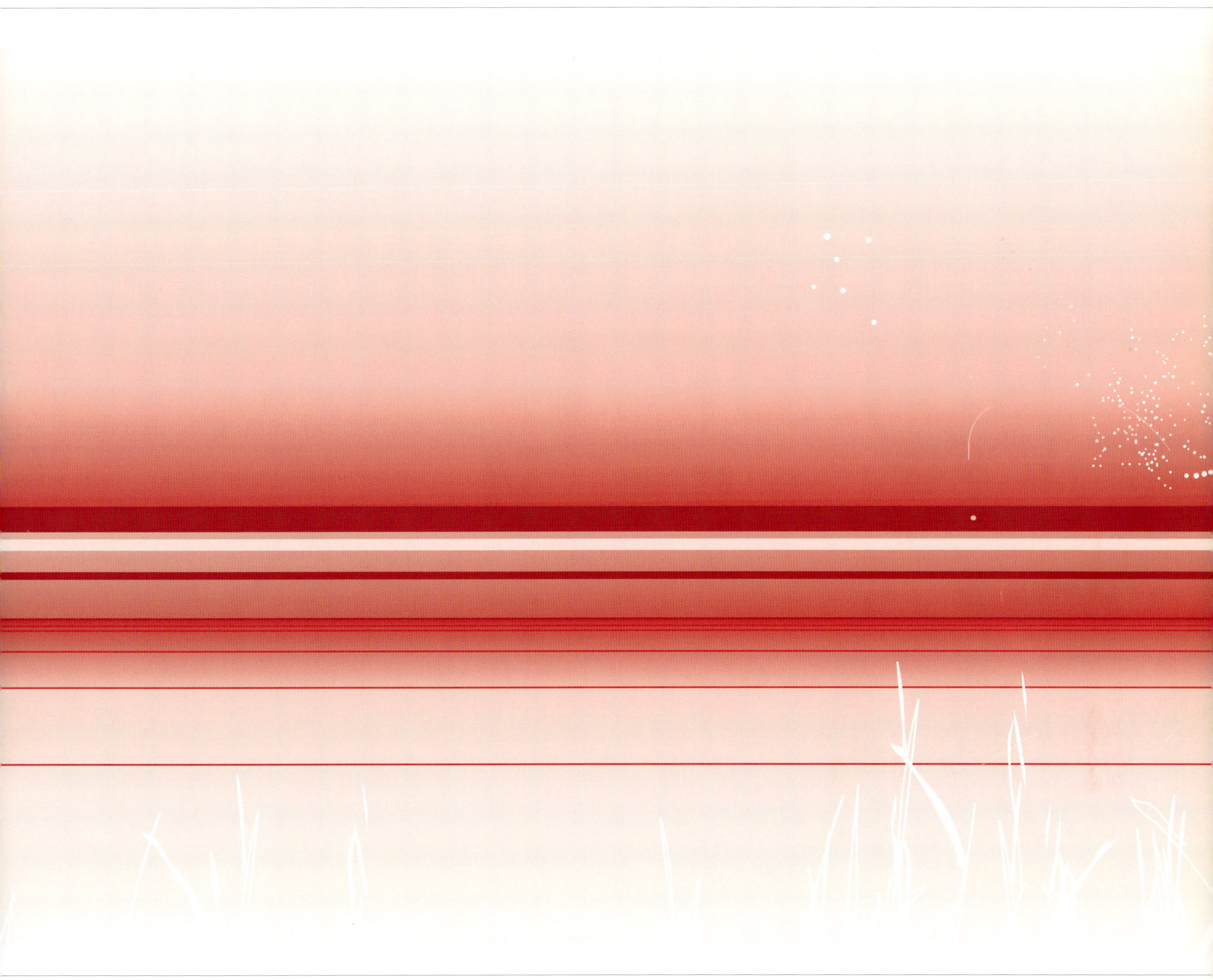

Design spreads for fashion lookbook. Illustrations by Adam Pointer

14 09

NOTHING

Still from McAlmont music promo

Virgin Records, images from international conference brochure and video

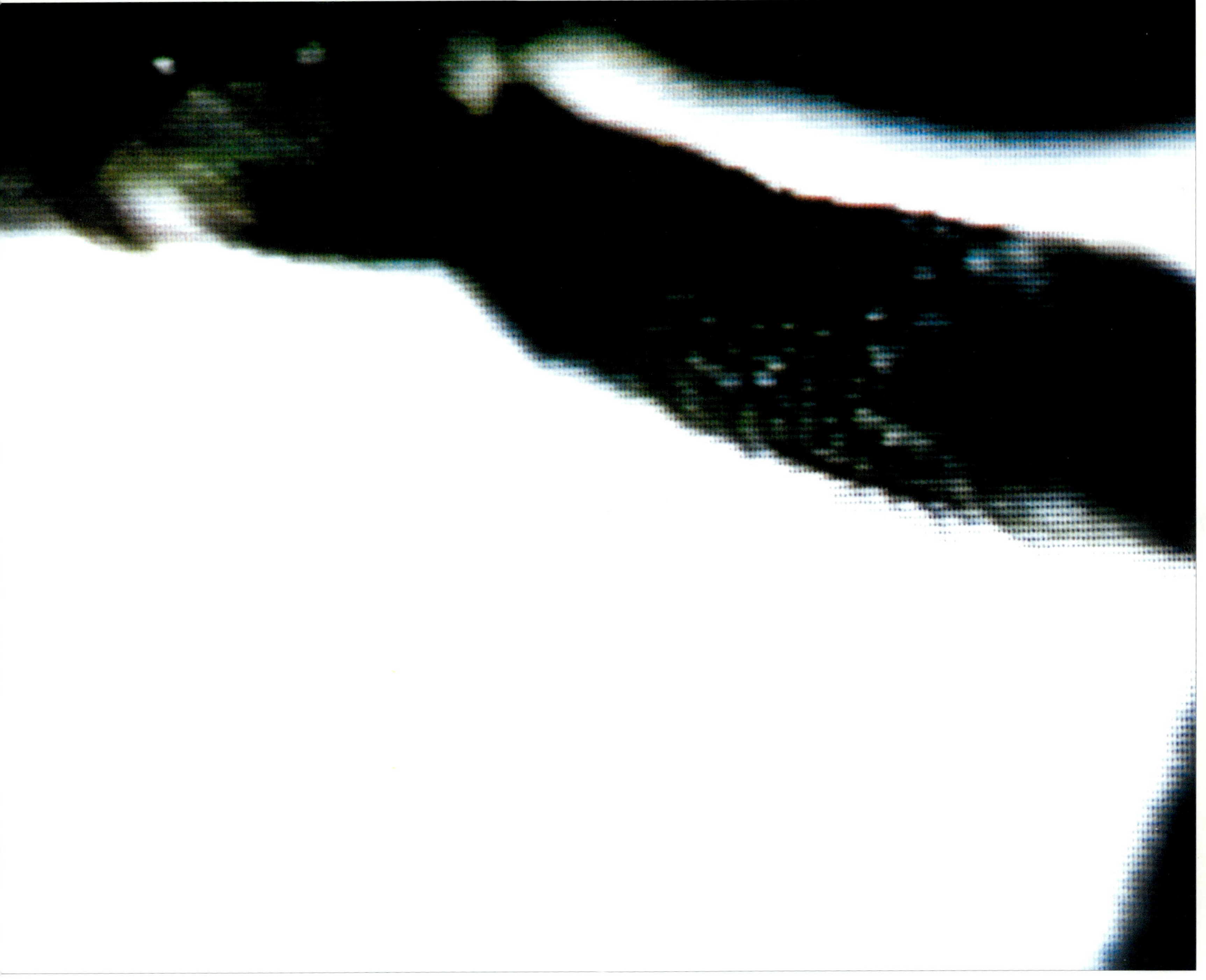

NO

I DON'T WANT
FF >>

NO MORE NO

YOU CAN
LOSE THE PAIN

In a side street near the office the parking meters had been beheaded or bent over at a right angle, and the parking signs were now bare poles. It was an empty street, being short and made up mainly of the backs of adjoining buildings, with one small warehouse, its shuttered façade sealed by rusty padlocks and the name painted above long illegible. There was a small pub as well, which looked as if it had last opened a couple of decades ago. But walk past at lunchtime – it was not a street to take after dark – and shadows moved behind the dirty frosted glass of the pub windows, noiselessly.

Turn out of the silent street at either end, and the traffic roared past, and beyond that the building cranes and cement mixers, scaffolding and dust showed where other remaining traces of the area's urban past were being pulled like rotten teeth, ready to implant health clubs and wine bars, internet cafes and – on one site – mini-lofts. What could a mini-loft be? Like a loft, but littler, one supposed. Take an idea from the old garment districts of southern Manhattan and transplant it across the Atlantic to London. And it shrank in the process, as London's garment district – for that had been one of the industries around here, as irony had it – had needed smaller, lower spaces. Whatever next: the twelve-storey skyscraper, the double bicycle car port perhaps.

It wasn't a new process, the American import. When the designer Raymond Loewy reopened his London office in 1949, he'd been summoned to meet the chairman of one of Britain's car companies, who had asked to be briefed on what was going on in American car design. Loewy, scenting a commission, told him what he knew, from his own work at Studebaker, and from the shows and Motoramas he had visited. 'Thank you,' said the chairman at the end in a patrician and satisfied voice, 'now I know just what to tell my chaps to do. Goodbye, Mr Loewy.' The result of all that was a car like the Morris 1000, that followed the curving forms of American bodywork but shrank it down – shrinking again – to a twelve foot chassis, not a twenty-foot one. The result, especially the half-timbered version, had a quaint, very English feel about it, as far away from Dearborn or Detroit as, well, a Cotswold village. Transport the American gangster film to London, around the same time, and it gets cloaked in the subtle charm of the Lady Killers or the Lavender Hill Mob.

But was that charm now going? The mini-loft was straight commercial cynicism, after all. Were the streets now to be mean streets, hard streets, the terrains of Hill Street Blues or Urban Cowboy? The streets of Victorian London had often been poor, and drowned in the fogs that charmed over Whistler's Chelsea riverscapes and terrified in Jack the Ripper's Whitechapel. But they had a human scale to them, a human presence – too much human presence and not enough soap or sewers, perhaps, as well. There was a certain resilience there that defeated meanness, against all the signs. Not just the 'chirpy Cockney sparrer' rubbish of wartime documentaries, either. But now?

Then, on the lost street, opposite the warehouse, there was something on the dirty, dank, blank brick wall. A neat, newly painted white square. On that, handlettered in black but in a passable imitation of official signage typography, the words: Please park anywhere you like. And underneath: By order. It was the last line that counted, that showed that humanity and wit was still at work, even here.

ordinary

exactly

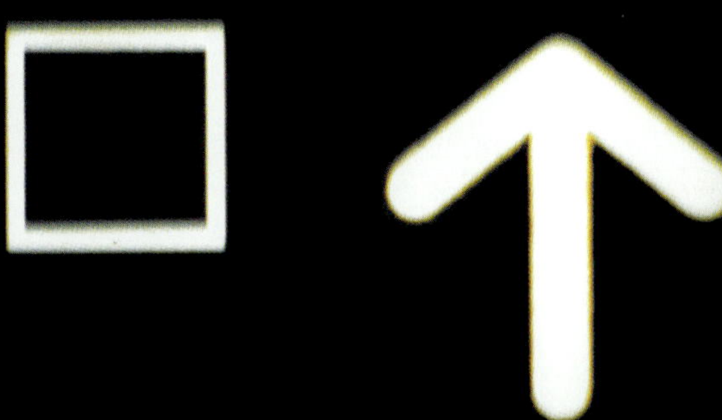

to be continued...

Editors
Petra Kiedaisch
Vineeta Manglani

Design and Art Direction
root
www.rootdesign.co.uk

Production
avcommunication AG

Printed by
Leibfarth & Schwarz,
Dettingen an der Erms

Die Deutsche Bibliothek - CIP-Einheitsaufnahme

root / Conway Lloyd Morgan. - Ludwigsburg: av-Ed., 2002 (av-Edition rockets)

ISBN 3-929638-62-2
Printed in Germany

Vega4
Photography by Lee Strickland
Satellite image by Jeremy Coysten
'Love Breaks Down' Lyrics by McDaid / Walker
'Drifting Away Violently' Lyrics by McDaid / Walker

The Specialists
Stand contractor Creator
Photography by Michael Donal

Dido TV commercial
Photography by Simon Emmett
Production Company Flynn Productions
Edit facility Soho 601

Orange Independent filmmakers event
Scripts and imagery supplied by
Independent filmmakers
Graphic panels Phillips Photographic

Soundscapes brochure
Photography by Kevin Griffin
Assisted by Tas Kyprianou
Musical Instruments supplied
by John Henry Enterprises

PlayStation
Stand contractor Mice
Advertising imagery and 'Mental Wealth'
poem supplied by TBWA Simons Palmer
Photography Dan Burn-Forti

Virgin Interactive Brochure
Photography by Mike Smith
Styling by Claire Todd
Hair and make-up by Carol Hart
Mannequins supplied by Adel Rootstein

SNK Advertising
Photography by Tom Dunkley
Many thanks to Steve 'Granada' man

Cold Turkey Project
Digital retouching Idea

Wamdue Project Music Promo
Production Company Flynn Productions

Fashion lookbook – Illustrations Adam Pointer

McAlmont Music Promo
Production Company Dreamchaser

Westlife
Photography by Sandrine Dulermo

root would like to thank the following companies, artists, designers and everyone who has contributed to this book:

BMG Entertainment
Virgin Records
Universal Records
Sony PlayStation Europe
Polydor Records
Orange
Taste Media
Capitol Records
Vega4
Séan Management
Virgin Interactive
Bastion PR
SNK
Dido
Cheeky Records
Flynn Productions Limited

Henry's House PR
Medal
RCA Records
Soundproof
Westlife
Sonny Takhar
Lee Strickland
Metro Imaging
Creator Construction Limited
Simon Emmett
Soho 601
Independent short filmmakers
Tas Kyprianou
19/20 Bar Clerkenwell
Phillips Photographic
Kevin Griffin

John Henry Enterprises
Mice
TBWA Simons Palmer
Dan Burn-Forti
Fran Cotton
Ron Adiello
Mike Smith
Adel Rootstein
Jonathan Rose
Tom Dunkley
Pico
GT Interactive
Heavy Pencil
Sandrine Dulermo
Jeremy Coyston
AMPM

Adam Pointer
David McAlmont
Dreamchaser Productions
QD Productions
FrameStore

All clients, designers, photographers, illustrators and suppliers who we have enjoyed working with.

Special thanks to Christopher Ringsell and Jennie Aldren

And in particular for Jo, George and Issy